THE CAST-IRON SKILLET COOKBOOK

THE CAST-IRON SKILLET COOKBOOK

A Tantalizing Collection of Over 200 Delicious Recipes for Every Kitchen

Dominique DeVito

KENNEBUNKPORT, MAINE

The Cast-Iron Skillet Cookbook

13-Digit ISBN: 978-1-60464-122-6
10-Digit ISBN: 1-60464-122-3

Appleseed Press Book Publishers
68 North Street
Kennebunkport, Maine 04046
Visit us online! appleseedpressbooks.com

Typography: Avenir, Fairfield, Fenway Park, Gotham, Journal, Linotype Centennial, Minion Pro
Image Credits: Page 96 © StockFood / Haigwood Studios; All other images used under official license from Shutterstock.com

Printed in China

1 2 3 4 5 6 7 8 9
First Edition

CONTENTS

Equipment: 12.5" skillet.

A 10-12" skillet may be used but cooking times will vary slightly.

THE CARE AND KEEPING OF YOUR CAST-IRON COOKWARE

We cooks have so many options when it comes to preparing foods: ovens, stoves, microwaves, grills, stainless steel, crockery, electric slow cookers, and woks. Among all these choices, a very old cooking tool—cast iron—is experiencing a renaissance of sorts in the modern kitchen. When you season and prep cast iron and start using it to make the delectable selection of recipes in this cookbook, you'll soon discover why it has stood the test of time—and is redefining the modern family's practices.

You may already be familiar with a cast-iron skillet. It's the plain, black, one-piece pan that always seemed to be at the back of the stack of fry pans in the cupboard. If you can remember where you saw that old pan, by all means, go get it. Acquiring a piece of cast-iron cookware from someone in your family is a way of keeping history alive. You'll be carrying on a tradition of cooking and serving foods that has been passed through generations. If, on the other hand, you're new to using cast iron and you are the one to acquire it in your family, you can look forward to sharing its results with your family and to someday passing it on to your children or grandchildren.

Besides being an amazing piece of cookware, cast-iron does, indeed, last a lifetime (or more)—so long as it's properly cared for. It's simple enough to do, but it's important to do it properly, not only before you use a pan for the first time but before and after every use. Here's how it is done.

SEASONING A NEW SKILLET

When I went shopping for a new cast-iron skillet, I came upon Lodge pans—a company that has been making cast-iron skillets since the late 1800s. They brand themselves as "America's Original Cookware." Since nothing stands completely still, they have recently developed a method to season their cookware so that it will last as it always has but with minimal (consistent) care. That's a good thing! What they do is coat the pan with vegetable oil and bake it in at very high heat, which is just what you need to do to an unseasoned pan. With a new Lodge seasoned piece, you can be cooking from it almost immediately.

But let's start at the beginning, with an unseasoned skillet. Here's the procedure to bring it into use:

1. Wash with hot, soapy water.
2. Rinse and dry thoroughly.
3. If there's any rust on the pan, sand it lightly with fine-grained sandpaper. Apply Coca-Cola to the rust spots and leave on for 10 to 15 minutes. Wash again with soapy water, rinse, dry and put the skillet on a burner over low heat to dry any excess moisture.
4. If there's no rust, after drying the cookware all over, apply a light layer of cooking oil (vegetable oil, NOT olive oil, butter, or margarine!) all over the pan with a paper towel, rubbing even the handle. The pan should have a light sheen to it.
5. Place the skillet upside down on the middle rack of the oven and preheat the oven to 400 degrees (with the pan inside). Put a piece of foil or a baking dish on the lower rack to catch any drips of oil. Let the pan cook in the oven for about 2 hours.
6. Turn the oven off and let the pan cool (upside down) in the oven.
7. Take it out, wipe it down with a clean paper towel, and it's good to go.
8. If your pan has taken on a slightly brown color, you can repeat the process, which will further season the pan and darken its color, improving its appearance. This will also happen over time.

CARING FOR YOUR CAST IRON

Rule #1: Never wash your seasoned pan with soapy water!

Rule #2: Never put a cast-iron pan in the dishwasher!

Why? Soap breaks down the protective seasoning, and you have to re-season the pan all over again. Leaving any kind of water on the pan will lead to rusting, which will demand re-seasoning from the beginning. It seems counter-intuitive, especially when you're used to thinking "it's not clean unless it's been washed in (really) hot, soapy water," but it's actually a great thing about cast iron.

After you've cooked in your skillet, clean it with hot water (no soap) and a plastic, rough-surfaced scrub brush. Dry the cookware completely (all over) after washing. Put a teaspoon of vegetable oil in the pan and, with a paper towel, rub it in all over the pan until it has a nice sheen. Take a fresh paper towel and wipe the cookware dry. Store it where there is good air circulation so no moisture is trapped on it. If you need to stack it, put paper towels on the top and bottom.

GIVE IT A LOT OF LOVE

The best thing to do with your cast-iron skillet is USE IT! When you start using it for all the different things it can do (as evidenced by the diversity of recipes in this book), you'll probably find that the skillet lives on your stovetop, waiting for its next assignment. The more you use it, the better it gets. Nothing will stick to its surface. You can go from the frying pan to the fire, as it were, starting a dish on the stove and finishing it in the oven. You can cook your skillet to a very high heat (or put it in the campfire), and it'll cook up the food you put in it beautifully (so long as you keep an eye on it).

In short, with regular use, the cast-iron skillet truly is a pan that will just keep cooking and cooking, getting better and better with age and use. Just like you and me!

BREAKFAST & BRUNCH

There's something about the very word *breakfast* that makes your mouth water in anticipation. The association with fried eggs, sizzling bacon, crisp-edged potatoes, butter melting over hot pancakes—flavors and aromas that jump-start your day and make you feel like you can tackle anything. Another reason a real breakfast is so satisfying is because it's not every day that we're able to indulge in it. Who has the time during the week to make pancakes—or even eggs? I suspect very few of us, which is why breakfast is particularly delicious and delightful when it can happen in our homes. The recipes in this chapter are what a good breakfast is all about—hearty, filling, hot, salty, sweet—or all of these things! Using a cast-iron skillet to cook breakfast also connects you to a feeling of tradition. You can imagine pioneers and homesteaders reaching for their skillets while wondering what was next for them as they headed West. You can imagine a farmer's wife cracking just-gathered eggs into a hot skillet in anticipation of her husband and children finishing the first round of milking and chores on the dairy farm. In our kitchens and lives, surrounded by the latest technology, there's nothing like breakfast prepared in a cast-iron skillet. So get cooking!

CHEESY SCRAMBLED EGGS

SERVES 2 ✦ ACTIVE TIME: 15 MINUTES ✦ START TO FINISH: 30 MINUTES

This is gooey goodness at its best. Well, you could always add bacon crumbles to take it way over the top, but the egg-and-cheese combo is pretty darn perfect in its simplicity.

2 tablespoons butter

6 large eggs

¼ cup heavy cream

1 cup shredded sharp cheddar cheese

½ teaspoon salt

Freshly ground black pepper

1. Heat the skillet over medium-high heat. Melt the butter in the skillet, being careful not to let it burn.
2. In a bowl, whisk the eggs until combined. Add the cream and whisk it into the eggs. Pour the egg mixture into the hot skillet. Using a wooden spoon, start to stir the eggs in the skillet as they start to cook. After a couple of minutes, turn the heat down to medium. Top the eggs with the cheese and stir it in as the eggs finish cooking. Be careful not to overcook the eggs.
3. Remove from heat, add salt and pepper, and serve immediately. Season with additional salt and pepper to taste.

Variations

- Use ¾ cup fresh mozzarella instead of cheddar.
- Use 1 cup Swiss cheese instead of cheddar.
- Use a cheese combo of ½ cup cheddar and ½ cup Swiss or Parmesan cheese.
- Add fresh herbs such as 1 teaspoon fresh basil, parsley, chives, or cilantro, or ½ teaspoon of rosemary.

TOMATO–MUSHROOM FRITTATA

SERVES 4 ✦ ACTIVE TIME: 20 MINUTES ✦ START TO FINISH: 40 MINUTES

Frittatas are like omelets in that they are combinations of eggs with other ingredients. The difference is that the frittata is like a crustless quiche, where the extras are cooked in with the eggs instead of being placed on top of an egg "pancake" and folded over. This one is especially yummy.

2 tablespoons butter

6 eggs

¼ cup milk or heavy cream

½ pound mushroom pieces, cleaned and sliced

1 large tomato, core and seeds removed, cut into small pieces

½ teaspoon salt

Freshly ground black pepper

¼ cup basil, coarsely chopped

½ to 1 teaspoon hot sauce, if desired

1. Preheat the broiler to low.
2. Heat the skillet on medium-high heat. Melt the butter in the skillet, being careful not to let it burn.
3. Whisk the eggs in a large bowl until combined. Add the milk or cream and stir. Add the mushroom pieces and tomatoes. Add the salt and pepper, and the hot sauce if desired.
4. Pour the egg mixture into the skillet. After a couple of minutes, as the eggs begin to set, sprinkle the basil over them. Lower the heat to medium or low, cover, and finish cooking until eggs are set, another 10 minutes. Place the skillet under the broiler for just a couple of minutes to "toast" the top.
5. Allow to sit for a few minutes. Season with additional salt and pepper, and serve.

A frittata is a great dish to take on a picnic as it is equally delicious served at room temperature. Serve with a nice green salad and a piece of crusty bread, and you'll have a first-class picnic.

SPINACH FRITTATA

SERVES 4 ✦ ACTIVE TIME: 20 MINUTES ✦ START TO FINISH: 30 MINUTES

This delicious combination gives a nod to Greek cuisine with the addition of feta cheese. Serve this for brunch with other classic Greek foods, like olives, pita wedges, and tzatziki sauce (recipe below).

6 eggs

2 tablespoons butter

¼ cup chopped red onion

1 clove garlic, minced

2 cups fresh spinach leaves, coarse stems removed, roughly chopped

½ cup feta cheese

Salt and pepper to taste

1. Preheat the broiler to low.
2. In a small bowl, beat the eggs with a whisk until combined.
3. Heat skillet over medium-high heat. Melt the butter in the skillet and add the onions and garlic, stirring to cook until onions are translucent, about 3 minutes.
4. Add the spinach and stir so the leaves wilt. Sprinkle the feta over the mixture.
5. Pour the eggs over everything and shake the pan to evenly distribute them. Sprinkle with salt and pepper. Cover the skillet and let cook until set, about 10 minutes. Place the skillet in the oven under the broiler to "toast" the top, about 2 minutes.
6. Allow to stand for a couple of minutes, and serve. Season with additional salt and pepper to taste.

Tzatziki Sauce is a simple blend of cucumbers, yogurt, garlic, and lemon juice, and it's a refreshing accompaniment to egg and meat dishes. To make it, peel, remove the seeds from and finely chop half of a cucumber. Wrap it in a cheesecloth or paper towel and squeeze it to get the juice out. Put the pieces in a bowl. Add 2 cups plain Greek yogurt, 2 tablespoons fresh-squeezed lemon juice, 4 cloves of garlic (pressed), and salt and pepper to taste. Refrigerate for at least 1 hour before serving, longer if possible. If desired, you can add fresh dill.

BACON AND EGGS

SERVES 2 ACTIVE TIME: 20 MINUTES START TO FINISH: 30 MINUTES

Done right, a simple dish of sizzling bacon accompanied by fried eggs, their yolks golden and gooey, is a plate of heaven on earth.

8 slices bacon

4 eggs

Heat a 12-inch skillet over medium-high heat. As it is heating, lay the bacon strips side by side in the skillet. Cook for about 5 minutes a side or until the meaty parts are cooked through and the fatty parts are opaque. If you prefer your bacon extra crispy, keep an eye on it as it continues to cook and allow it to go another few minutes, turning after every couple of minutes.

Transfer the cooked bacon to a plate lined with paper towels, and keep it in a warm oven. Drain most of the fat from the skillet, but keep enough to coat the bottom.

The skillet should be hot from having just made the bacon. Crack the eggs into the sizzling bacon fat. Lower the heat to medium or low, and put a lid over the skillet for about 2 minutes to help cook the yolk without overdoing the white.

When the eggs are cooked, remove with a spatula and serve immediately, accompanied by the bacon.

We owe our American traditional breakfast of bacon and eggs to our English ancestors. A full English breakfast consists of eggs, sausage, potatoes, and even baked beans and tomatoes, all washed down with strong tea or coffee.

VEGETABLE FRITTATA

SERVES 4 ✦ ACTIVE TIME: 20 MINUTES ✦ START TO FINISH: 40 MINUTES

Make this veggie-loaded egg dish as a hearty breakfast or a light dinner. It's a perfect thing to cook up with fresh ingredients bought at the local farmer's market.

6 eggs

3 tablespoons butter

½ onion, minced

2 cloves garlic, minced

2 carrots, sliced thin

½ small zucchini, sliced thin

½ red pepper, seeded and sliced thin

⅓ cup parsley, chopped fine

Salt and pepper to taste

1 teaspoon red pepper flakes, if desired

1. Preheat the broiler to low.
2. In a bowl, whisk the eggs until combined.
3. Heat the skillet over medium-high heat. Melt the butter in the skillet. Add the onions and garlic and cook, stirring, until onions are translucent, about 3 minutes.
4. Add the carrots and zucchini slices, lower the heat to medium, and cook, stirring occasionally, until softened, about 5 minutes. Add the red pepper and continue to cook, about 5 minutes. Add the parsley.
5. Pour the eggs over the vegetables. Shake the skillet to distribute evenly. Season with salt and pepper, and sprinkle with red pepper flakes if desired. Cover and cook until eggs are set, about 10 minutes.
6. Put the skillet in the oven and cook for a few minutes to "toast" the top. Remove from the oven and let sit for a few minutes before serving.

There are so many delicious ingredients in this frittata that it's practically a one-pan meal. Make it even heartier by adding sweet potatoes. Wash a large sweet potato and pierce it all over with a fork. Put it on a paper towel in the microwave and cook for 3 minutes. Using a dish towel because it will be hot, turn the potato over and cook another 2 or 3 minutes. Allow to cool for a minute or so, and cut the potato into bite-sized pieces. Add it to the frittata after the red peppers.

HAM, HERB, AND TOMATO FRITTATA

SERVES 4 ✦ ACTIVE TIME: 20 MINUTES ✦ START TO FINISH: 40 MINUTES

Smoked ham provides an earthiness to this baked egg dish, which is also loaded with fresh herbs and dotted with tomatoes.

2 tablespoons butter

½ pound thick-sliced deli ham, cut into pieces

6 eggs

¼ cup milk or heavy cream

1 teaspoon salt

Freshly ground black pepper

6 cherry tomatoes, cut in half

½ cup fresh parsley, coarsely chopped

1 teaspoon fresh thyme, minced

1. Preheat the broiler to low.
2. Heat the skillet on medium-high heat. Melt the butter in the skillet, being careful not to let it burn. Add the ham to the pan and stir, cooking until just browned, about 3 minutes.
3. Whisk the eggs in a large bowl until combined. Add the milk or cream and stir. Add the salt and pepper.
4. Pour the egg mixture into the skillet. After a couple of minutes, as the eggs begin to set, add the cherry tomato halves and sprinkle the herbs over everything. Lower the heat to medium or low, cover, and finish cooking until eggs are set, another 10 minutes. Place the skillet under the broiler for just a couple of minutes to "toast" the top.
5. Allow to sit for a few minutes. Season with additional salt and pepper, if desired, and serve.

This is one of those frittatas into which you could add almost anything tasty in the fridge. Substitute cooked chicken pieces for the ham; sprinkle leftover sautéed greens over the eggs; add some chopped jalapenos for extra flavor and heat. Have fun experimenting.

SMOKED SALMON FRITTATA

SERVES 4 ✦ ACTIVE TIME: 20 MINUTES ✦ START TO FINISH: 30 MINUTES

Salmon is a high-protein, low-fat food that adds lots of flavor, texture, and—best of all—taste! Combined with the almost sweetness of leeks, this recipe is one you'll want to use for a special brunch.

2 leeks, white part only

2 tablespoons olive oil

1 tablespoon butter

8 eggs

½ cup cream or half-and-half

1 teaspoon salt

Ground pepper to taste

4 oz. smoked salmon, chopped

3-oz. package cream cheese, softened and cut into bits

1. Preheat the broiler to low.
2. Slice the white parts of the leeks into thin slices. Put them in a colander, separating the circles. Rinse thoroughly to be sure there is no fine dirt or sand. Dry the leeks in paper towels.
3. Heat the oil with the butter in the skillet over medium-high heat. Add the leeks and cook, stirring, until translucent and tender, 3 to 5 minutes. Reduce the heat to low.
4. In a bowl, whisk the eggs until well blended, and add the cream, salt, and pepper. Pour the eggs over the leeks in the skillet and increase heat to medium. Place pieces of salmon and cream cheese on top of the eggs. Cover the skillet and let cook until set, about 10 minutes. Place the skillet in the oven under the broiler to "toast" the top, about 2 minutes.

If you like dill, it makes an excellent garnish for this very tasty frittata. Finely chop some sprigs and sprinkle them over the dish when it is cool. Another tasty addition is pieces of steamed asparagus, which can be sprinkled throughout at the same time as the fish and cream cheese.

MAINLY MUSHROOM FRITTATA

SERVES 4 ✦ ACTIVE TIME: 20 MINUTES ✦ START TO FINISH: 40 MINUTES

If you love mushrooms (and I sure do!), you'll love this frittata. The mushrooms are moist and earthy, the perfect base for the Swiss cheese and eggs.

3 tablespoons butter

½ onion, diced

1 pound mushrooms, picked over and sliced or chopped

1 teaspoon salt

½ teaspoon pepper

1 tablespoon dry Vermouth (optional)

8 eggs

½ cup milk or half-and-half

1 cup Swiss cheese, shredded

⅓ cup fresh parsley, chopped

1. Melt the butter in the skillet over medium-high heat. Add the onions and cook, stirring, until translucent, about 3 minutes. Add the mushrooms, lower the heat slightly, and cook, stirring occasionally, until soft, 5 to 10 minutes. Drain the liquid from the pan. Season the mushrooms with the salt and pepper, and add the Vermouth if desired.
2. In a bowl, whisk the eggs with the milk. Pour the egg mixture over the mushrooms. Sprinkle the cheese all around the top, and then sprinkle the parsley over everything. Cover the skillet and let cook until set, about 10 minutes. Place the skillet in the oven under the broiler and "toast" the top, about 2 minutes.

The selection of mushrooms in grocery stores is getting bigger and bigger. You can use one kind of mushroom for this dish, or you can use several kinds together. For example, you could use sliced white mushrooms, and you won't need to do much prep work with them. Or you could choose Portobellos, which have a meatier texture and flavor. There are also shiitake or cremini mushrooms. If you mix the mushrooms, just be sure to cut them into similarly sized pieces so they cook evenly.

BEST-EVER HASHED BROWNS

SERVES 4 TO 6 ✦ ACTIVE TIME: 40 MINUTES ✦ START TO FINISH: 60 MINUTES

I always ask for crispy hash browns when I order them in a diner because I love when the outside is crisp and browned and the inside is soft and hot. Even your favorite diner's preparation won't match this recipe, though.

4 large russet potatoes

1 yellow onion

1 teaspoon salt

½ teaspoon pepper, or to taste

4 tablespoons butter

1. Peel the potatoes and wash them to remove any dirt from the potato or your hands. Grate the potatoes using the large holes of a cheese grater. Put the grated potatoes in a mixing bowl.
2. Cut the onion in half, and using the fine holes of the cheese grater, grate the cut side of the onion over the potatoes so that some particles and juice go into the bowl. Don't overdo the onion; a couple of swipes over the grater is a good start. Thoroughly combine the potatoes and onion.
3. Squeeze the grated vegetables through a cheesecloth or in some paper towels. You want to get them as dry as possible. Stir in the salt and pepper.
4. Heat the butter in the skillet over medium-high heat until bubbling. Add the potatoes, pressing the mixture into the bottom of the pan to form a large pancake. Cook for 4 to 5 minutes on one side, then flip the potatoes and cook for another 3 minutes or more on the other side, depending on how crisp you want the potatoes. If you want to cook them a little longer, consider adding some more butter to the pan, one tablespoon at a time.
5. Serve hot, seasoning with additional salt and pepper if desired.

If you have a food processer, you can use the shredding blade instead of using a cheese grater for the potatoes. The finer your shreds, the faster the potatoes will cook. Consider cooking them in bacon grease instead of butter for added flavor, or you can substitute olive oil for the butter (but in my opinion it doesn't taste as good).

POTATOES, PEPPERS, AND EGGS

SERVES 4 TO 6 ✦ ACTIVE TIME: 20 MINUTES ✦ START TO FINISH: 40 MINUTES

This is a fun dish to make for company on a weekend morning. It's easy, and it makes a great presentation.

1 tablespoon olive oil

1 red pepper, cored and chopped

¼ onion, diced

Red pepper flakes (optional)

4 large russet potatoes, shredded with a cheese grater and squeezed dry

1 teaspoon salt

½ teaspoon pepper, or to taste

4 tablespoons butter

6 eggs

1. Heat the oil in the skillet over medium-high heat. Add the pepper and onion and cook, stirring, until softened and just darkening on the outside, about 4 minutes. Stir in the red pepper flakes if desired. Stir the pepper/onion mix into the shredded potatoes. Season with salt and pepper.
2. Add the butter to the skillet, and when bubbling, add the potatoes, pressing into the bottom of the pan. Cook for about 5 minutes.
3. Create six indentations in the potatoes and break the eggs into them (one egg per indentation). Reduce the heat slightly, cover, and continue to cook until the whites of the eggs are cooked through and the yolks are set, about 5 minutes. Serve immediately.

Red peppers are a bit milder than green peppers. You can substitute a green pepper if desired, or use a combination. Instead of adding red pepper flakes, if you want a little fire in your dish, add a teaspoon of chopped, seeded jalapeno pepper with the red or green pepper (and onion).

CHEESY HASH BROWNS

SERVES 4 TO 6 ✦ ACTIVE TIME: 20 MINUTES ✦ START TO FINISH: 60 MINUTES

If you want gooey goodness without the fat from meat, this recipe is for you. Be careful not to overcook it or you'll go from gooey to chewy (which isn't bad, either).

4 tablespoons butter

4 large russet potatoes, shredded with a cheese grater and squeezed dry

1 teaspoon salt

½ teaspoon pepper, or to taste

6 eggs

½ cup milk

1 cup shredded cheese

1. Preheat the oven to 375 degrees.
2. Add the butter to the skillet, and when bubbling, add the potatoes and season with the salt and pepper. Press the potatoes into the bottom of the pan. Cook for about 5 minutes.
3. In a mixing bowl, whisk the eggs and milk together. Pour the eggs over the potatoes, shaking the pan to help them penetrate to the bottom. Sprinkle liberally with the cheese.
4. Transfer the skillet to the oven and cook until just set, about 10 minutes. Serve immediately.

The best cheeses to use in this recipe are those that melt well. This includes cheddar, Swiss, American, mozzarella, Monterey Jack, or Provolone. Use a blend of these cheeses if you want, so long as they are all shredded.

STICKY BUNS

SERVES 6 ✦ ACTIVE TIME: 90 MINUTES ✦ START TO FINISH: 2 HOURS

This takes a bit of preparation time, but the result is sooo worth it! Your family or friends will wake up to the smell of these baking, and you'll soon have a kitchen full of people happily waiting for these to come out of the oven.

26.4-oz. package frozen biscuits

All-purpose flour for dusting

½ cup chopped pecans, toasted

1 teaspoon ground cinnamon

¼ teaspoon nutmeg

4 tablespoons butter, softened

¾ cup firmly packed light brown sugar

1 cup confectioner's sugar

3 tablespoons half-and-half

½ teaspoon vanilla extract

1. Preheat oven to 375 degrees.
2. Lightly dust a flat surface with flour. Spread the frozen biscuit dough out in rows of 4 biscuits each. Cover with a dish cloth and let sit for about 30 minutes until the dough is thawed but still cool.
3. While dough is thawing, toast the pecans. Spread the pieces on a cookie sheet and bake for about 5 minutes, stirring the pieces with a spatula about halfway through. Be sure not to overcook. Allow to cool. Put the pieces in a bowl and add the cinnamon and nutmeg, stirring to coat the nuts with the spices.
4. Sprinkle flour over the top of the biscuit dough, and fold the dough in half, then press it out to form a large rectangle (approximately 10 inches by 12 inches). Spread the softened butter over the dough.
5. Sprinkle the brown sugar over the butter, then the seasoned nuts. Roll the dough with the butter, sugar, and nuts in it, starting with a long side. Cut into 1-inch slices and place in a lightly greased skillet.
6. Bake at 375 degrees for about 35 minutes, until rolls in the center are cooked through. Remove from the oven and allow to cool.
7. Make the glaze by mixing the confectioner's sugar, half-and-half, and vanilla. Drizzle over the warm rolls and serve.

Variations

- Substitute toasted walnut or almond pieces for the pecans for a nuttier, earthier flavor.
- Substitute dark brown sugar for the light brown sugar if you want more of a molasses flavor.
- Save a few calories (not many!) by using low-fat milk instead of half-and-half, or skip the glaze entirely and either serve without it or drizzle some maple syrup over the rolls.

THE DAVID EYRE PANCAKE

SERVES 4 ✦ ACTIVE TIME: 30 MINUTES ✦ START TO FINISH: 30 MINUTES

A friend shared this recipe that she found in the New York Times *years ago. Turns out it has quite the following. It's more like a popover than a pancake, but it's really delicious. David Eyre was a writer/editor, so I'm happy to include this tribute to him and hopefully create a whole new following for it.*

½ cup flour

½ cup milk

2 eggs, lightly beaten

Pinch of nutmeg

4 tablespoons butter

2 tablespoons confectioner's sugar

Juice of half a lemon

1. Preheat oven to 425 degrees.
2. In a bowl, combine the flour, milk, eggs, and nutmeg. Beat lightly; leave the batter a little lumpy.
3. Melt the butter in the skillet and, when very hot, pour in the batter.
4. Transfer the skillet to the oven and bake for 15 to 20 minutes, until golden brown.
5. Sprinkle with the sugar, return briefly to the oven, then remove, sprinkle with lemon juice, and serve.

This "pancake" is usually served with jam, which leads to all kinds of flavor options: Try anything from a sweet strawberry jam to a more pungent orange marmalade or fig spread. In the fall, an apple or pear butter would be perfect.

BLUEBERRY SCONES

MAKES A DOZEN SCONES ✦ ACTIVE TIME: 30 MINUTES ✦ START TO FINISH: 50 MINUTES

These are delicious whenever you eat them, but they're especially good about 15 minutes after you take them out of the oven, slathered with butter!

3 cups flour

⅓ cup sugar

2½ teaspoons baking powder

½ teaspoon baking soda

1 teaspoon salt

¾ cup (1½ sticks) unsalted butter, chilled and cut into pieces

1 tablespoon orange zest

1 cup milk or half-and-half

1 cup fresh blueberries

1. Preheat oven to 400 degrees. Position a rack in the middle of the oven.
2. In a large bowl, whisk together the flour, sugar, baking powder, baking soda, and salt. Add the butter pieces and mix with an electric mixer until just blended or mix with a fork so that the dough is somewhat crumbly.
3. Stir in the orange zest and milk, and gently fold in the blueberries, being careful not to overmix.
4. With flour on your hands, transfer the dough to a lightly floured surface. Form the dough into a circle about ½-inch thick. With a long knife, cut the dough into 12 wedges.
5. Butter the cast-iron skillet, and put the scone wedges in a circle in it, leaving some space between the pieces. Bake for 20 to 25 minutes, or until golden.
6. If desired, sprinkle with some additional sugar when just out of the oven.

Blueberries split when cooked and their juices can get a little messy. If you want a neater-looking scone, you can use dried blueberries. Reduce the amount used by about half, though, as their flavor is also more concentrated.

SAVORY SCONES

SERVES 4 TO 6 ✦ ACTIVE TIME: 30 MINUTES ✦ START TO FINISH: 50 MINUTES

These cheesy scones with extra black pepper are a nice complement to scrambled eggs. You can also split them and use them as sandwich bread for a ham-and-egg breakfast sandwich. Or enjoy them in the afternoon with a cup of tea.

2 cups flour

1 teaspoon baking powder

½ teaspoon salt

1 teaspoon freshly ground black pepper

½ teaspoon dry mustard

4 tablespoons butter, chilled, cut into pieces

½ cup grated sharp cheddar cheese

½ cup milk

1 egg beaten with a little milk

1. Preheat oven to 400 degrees. Position a rack in the middle of the oven.
2. In a large bowl, whisk together the flour, baking powder, salt, pepper, and dry mustard. Add the butter pieces and mix with a fork to form a crumbly dough.
3. Stir in the cheese and milk. With flour on your hands, transfer the dough to a lightly floured surface.
4. Form the dough into a circle about ½-inch thick. With a long knife, cut the dough into 6 to 8 wedges.
5. Butter the skillet, and put the scone wedges in a circle in it, leaving some space between the pieces.
6. Brush with the beaten egg. Bake for 20 to 25 minutes, or until golden.

For an added breakfast treat, include bacon bits in the dough. Add about 1/3 cup crumbled bacon or bacon bits to the dough when adding the cheese and milk.

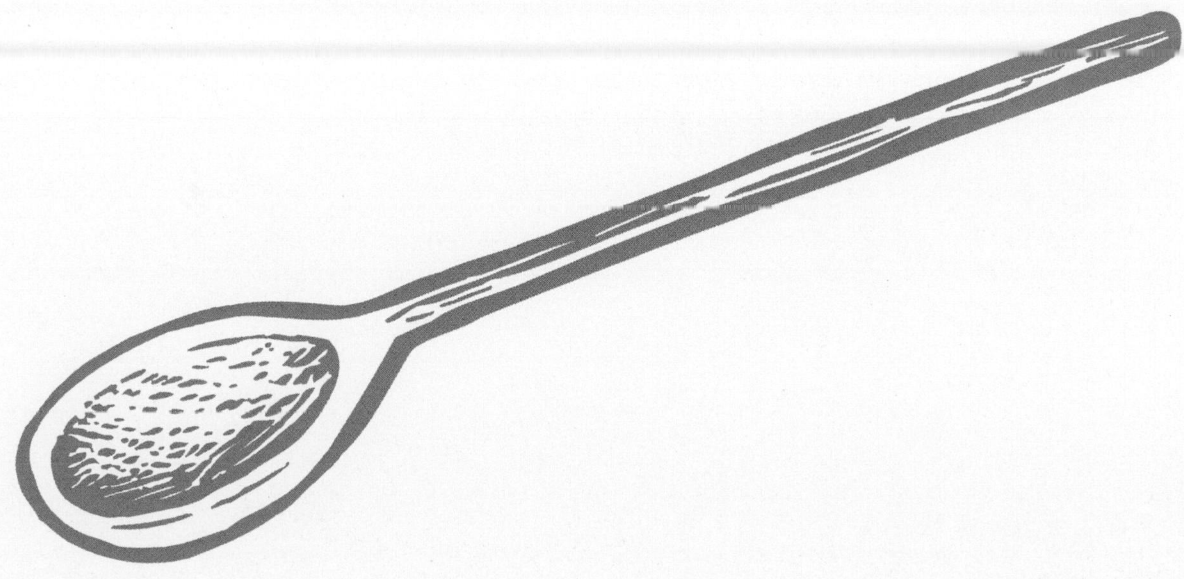

FRENCH TOAST

SERVES 3 TO 6 ✦ ACTIVE TIME: 20 MINUTES ✦ START TO FINISH: 40 MINUTES

French toast—a great way to use up bread that's on the verge of going stale—is so simple and so satisfying.

6 eggs

1 cup milk

½ teaspoon vanilla extract

Pinch of nutmeg, if desired

6 slices thick-cut bread

4 to 6 tablespoons butter

1. In a mixing bowl, combine the eggs, milk, vanilla, and nutmeg (if desired).
2. Place the slices of bread in a baking dish. Pour the egg mixture over the bread, shaking the pan to distribute evenly. Flip the pieces of bread a couple of times to coat both sides with the mixture.
3. Heat 2 tablespoons butter in the skillet over medium-high heat. Add 2 slices of bread to the pan and cook until golden brown on each side, 2 to 3 minutes a side. Transfer the cooked pieces to a warm plate or keep warm in the oven while you cook the additional pieces.
4. Serve with maple syrup or jam.

The secret to great French toast is the choice of bread and the amount of egg mixture that saturates the bread. If you use a basic sandwich bread, you won't need as much egg mixture. If you use an egg-based bread like Challah, or a sourdough bread, you'll need more egg mixture as these kinds of bread are denser. They will also need to sit in the egg mixture longer. You'll need to adjust the recipe for the type of bread you're using, so be sure to have some extra eggs and milk on hand.

PIG-AND-POTATO DELIGHT

SERVES 4 TO 6 ✦ ACTIVE TIME: 30 MINUTES ✦ START TO FINISH: 60 MINUTES

This is inspired by the men in our family, who can't seem to get enough meat with their eggs in the morning. It's a great one-pan meal, especially in winter, when you're looking for a hearty breakfast to start the day.

4 slices bacon

6 to 8 breakfast sausages (plain or maple), frozen

2 tablespoons butter

4 large russet potatoes, shredded with a cheese grater and squeezed dry

1 teaspoon salt

½ teaspoon pepper, or to taste

1. Heat the skillet over medium-high heat. Cook the bacon so that it's crispy, about 3 minutes a side.
2. Transfer the bacon slices to a plate lined with a paper towel. Put the sausages in the skillet with the bacon grease and reduce the heat to medium. Cook, stirring frequently, as the sausages start to thaw.
3. Cut into small pieces with a fork and continue to cook until the sausages are cooked through, about 10 minutes. Transfer the pieces to the plate with the bacon. Reduce the heat under the skillet to low.
4. Mix the sausage pieces in with the shredded potatoes, then crumble the bacon into the potatoes.
5. Turn the heat back up to medium high, and add the butter. When the butter is melted and bubbling with the bacon and sausage grease, add the potato-meat mixture. Press the shredded potatoes into the bottom of the pan. Cook for about 4 minutes on one side, then flip and continue to cook for another 4 or 5 minutes on the other side, until potatoes are crispy on the bottom and top and cooked through. Serve immediately.

This dish is also delicious with some onions and peppers. Use about 1/4 cup of each, chopped fine, and cook in the grease of the meats. Stir into the shredded potatoes with the meats and cook as directed above. Serve with hot sauce!

EGGS IN A NEST

SERVES 2 ACTIVE TIME: 20 MINUTES START TO FINISH: 40 MINUTES

This is a dish that's as much about presentation as it is about taste, but both are fabulous. It's guaranteed to put a smile on your child's face in the morning.

4 pieces of sandwich bread

4 tablespoons butter

4 eggs

Salt and pepper to taste

Using cookie cutters of different shapes can be fun and festive, too.

Toast the bread on the light setting of the toaster, until it is just browned. Using a cookie cutter or the top of a small glass, perforate a hole in the center of the piece of toast.

Heat 2 tablespoons of the butter in the skillet over medium-high heat. Put two pieces of the toast with the holes in it in the pan. Cook for a couple of minutes on one side to get them golden, then flip the toasts.

Crack the eggs into the holes. Lower the heat slightly, cover the pan, and cook until the egg is set, about 3 minutes. Serve the cooked pieces and repeat the cooking process with the other pieces of toast and eggs. Season with salt and pepper before serving.

CHEESY GRITS

SERVES 4 TO 6 ACTIVE TIME: 20 MINUTES START TO FINISH: 40 MINUTES

Done right, grits are a mouthful of special. No wonder they're a regular on the breakfast plates of Southerners.

2 cups whole milk

2 cups water

1 cup grits

1 teaspoon salt

1 teaspoon pepper

2 cups grated cheddar cheese (packed)

Preheat the broiler to high.

Bring the milk and water to a boil. Add the grits and stir, cooking constantly, until grits are thickened and cooked, about 15 minutes. Add the salt and pepper and 1 cup of the cheese. Stir to combine.

Grease the skillet with some butter and add the grits. Sprinkle with the remaining cup of cheese. Put the skillet in the oven and allow to toast under the broiler, about 2 minutes. Serve immediately.

If you want spicier grits, use 1 cup Monterey Jack cheese as half of the cheese you include. Or try other hard cheeses like Swiss, mozzarella, or fresh Parmesan.

CINNAMON BUNS

SERVES 6 ✦ ACTIVE TIME: 60 MINUTES ✦ START TO FINISH: 90 MINUTES

There's something about serving these fresh out of the skillet that makes them even more special than they already are. If you love the smell (and taste) of cinnamon, you will gobble these up.

26.4-oz. package(s) frozen biscuits

All-purpose flour for dusting

2 teaspoons ground cinnamon

¾ cup firmly packed dark brown sugar

4 tablespoons butter, softened

1 cup confectioner's sugar

3 tablespoons half-and-half

½ teaspoon vanilla extract

1. Preheat oven to 375 degrees.
2. Lightly dust a flat surface with flour. Spread the frozen biscuit dough out in rows of 4 biscuits each. Cover with a dish cloth and let sit for about 30 minutes until the dough is thawed but still cool.
3. Mix the cinnamon and brown sugar in a small bowl.
4. When the dough is ready, sprinkle flour over the top and fold it in half, then press it out to form a large rectangle (approximately 10x12 inches). Spread the softened butter over the dough, then the cinnamon/sugar mix. Roll up the dough, starting with a long side. Cut into 1-inch slices and place in a lightly greased skilled.
5. Bake at 375 degrees for about 35 minutes, until rolls in the center are cooked through. Remove from the oven and allow to cool slightly.
6. Make the glaze by mixing the confectioner's sugar, half-and-half, and vanilla. Drizzle over the warm rolls and serve.

Cinnamon is a spice with a long history of health benefits as well as culinary delights. The cinnamon sticks sold in stores are actually "quills" from cinnamon trees; they're the inner bark. Cinnamon is grown in India, Sri Lanka, Indonesia, Madagascar, Brazil, and parts of the Caribbean. Its smell is said to invigorate cognitive functions, and its compounds have antibacterial and analgesic properties. Cinnamon is used in both sweet and savory dishes.

CAST-IRON TIPS

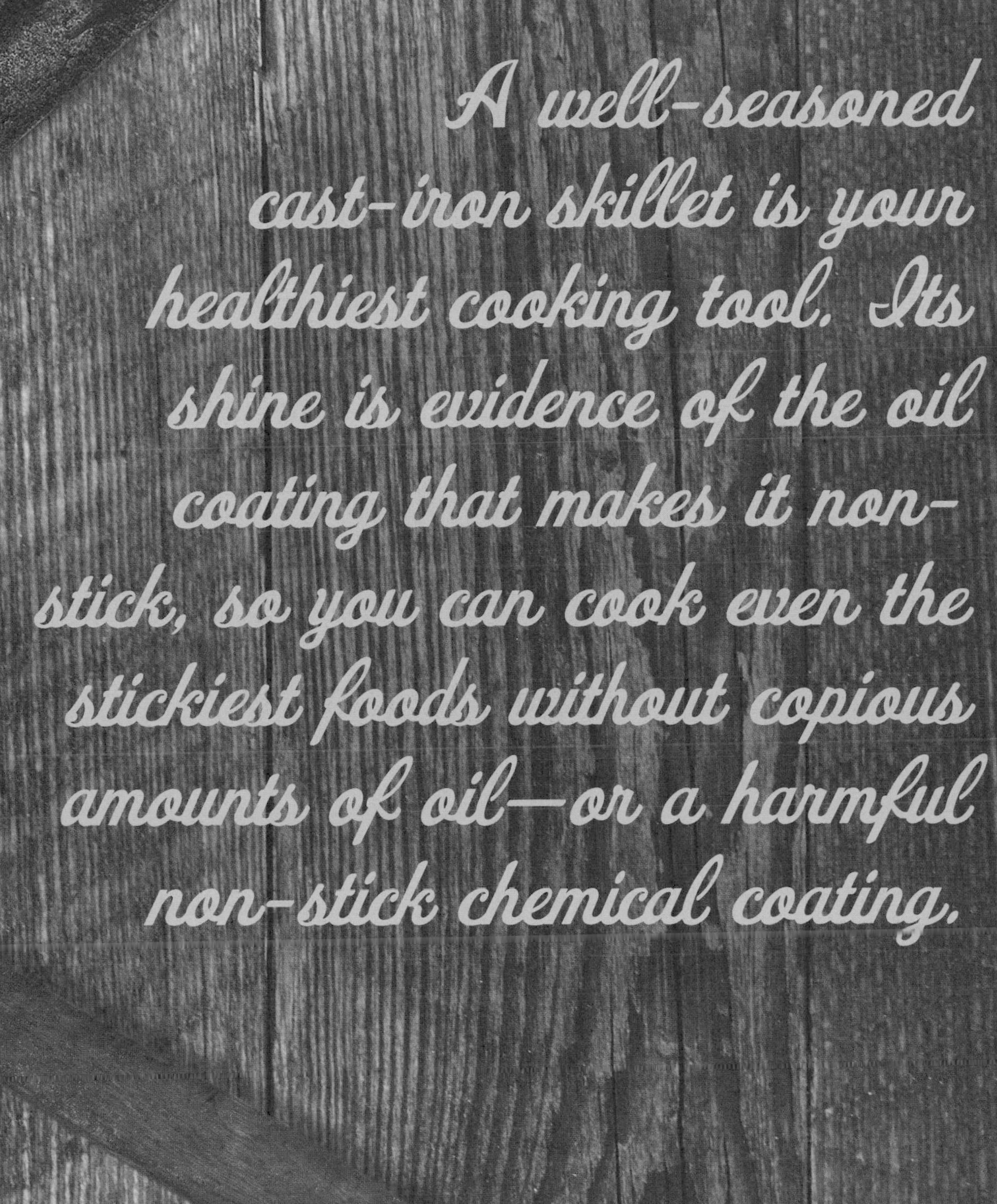

A well-seasoned cast-iron skillet is your healthiest cooking tool. Its shine is evidence of the oil coating that makes it non-stick, so you can cook even the stickiest foods without copious amounts of oil—or a harmful non-stick chemical coating.

BLINIS

SERVES 6 TO 8 ✦ ACTIVE TIME: 60 MINUTES ✦ START TO FINISH: 60 MINUTES

These Russian pancakes are traditionally served with sour cream and caviar. But they make great "fancy" breakfast pancakes that can be served with all sorts of different toppings, both sweet and savory.

½ cup whole wheat flour

1 tablespoon sugar

¼ teaspoon salt

½ teaspoon baking powder

2 eggs, beaten

2½ cups milk

2 tablespoons vegetable oil

1. In a large bowl, whisk together the flour, sugar, salt, and baking powder.
2. In a smaller bowl, combine the eggs and milk, stirring to combine. Add the liquid into the dry ingredients and stir to blend thoroughly.
3. Heat a skillet over medium-high heat and brush with some of the vegetable oil. Spoon just about a tablespoon of batter to form each blini. You should be able to fit about 4 at a time in the skillet. Cook for about 2 minutes a side (or less), flipping when the edges start to crisp. These cook up fast, so be careful not to overcook them.
4. Keep the blini warm in the oven on very low heat until ready to serve.

If you like caviar of any kind, you have to try these with a dollop of sour cream or crème fraiche topped with caviar. Other great toppings include assorted jams; sour cream with a sprig of dill; scrambled eggs and hot sauce; scrambled eggs, bacon bits, and sour cream; honey-butter.

SKILLET APPLE PANCAKE

SERVES 4 TO 6 ✦ ACTIVE TIME: 30 MINUTES ✦ START TO FINISH: 60 MINUTES

Make this the morning after you go apple picking. It's a great way to use up some of the apples and get your day off to a great start.

4 eggs

1 cup milk

3 tablespoons sugar

½ teaspoon vanilla

½ teaspoon salt

¾ cup flour

4 tablespoons butter

2 apples, peeled, cored and thinly sliced

¼ teaspoon cinnamon

Dash of ground nutmeg

Dash of ground ginger

¼ cup light brown sugar

Confectioner's sugar for sprinkling (optional)

1. Preheat the oven to 425 degrees.
2. In a large bowl, whisk together the eggs, milk, sugar, vanilla, and salt. Add the flour and whisk to combine. Set the batter aside.
3. Heat the skillet over medium-high heat and add the butter, tilting the pan to thoroughly coat the bottom. Add the apple slices and top with the cinnamon, nutmeg, and ginger. Stir, cooking, until apples begin to soften, about 5 minutes. Add the brown sugar and continue to stir while cooking for an additional few minutes until apples are very soft. Pat the cooked apples along the bottom of the skillet to distribute evenly.
4. Pour the batter over the apples, coating them evenly. Transfer the skillet to the oven and bake for about 20 minutes until it is browned and puffed. Sprinkle with confectioner's sugar when fresh out of the oven if desired. Serve immediately.

You can vary the fruit-spice combo for this recipe in multiple ways. Consider making it with pears instead of apples, or using one of each. Add raisins to the apples or pears while cooking (about 1/2 cup), or try cranberries, blueberries, or dried cherries, along with toasted walnuts (about 1/2 cup).

CORN CAKES

SERVES 4 ✦ ACTIVE TIME: 30 MINUTES ✦ START TO FINISH: 60 MINUTES

These breakfast treats are grittier and mealier than fluffy wheat-flour pancakes. But with pats of butter melted on top, they are even tastier!

1 cup yellow cornmeal

½ cup whole wheat flour

3 tablespoons sugar

1 tablespoon baking powder

¼ teaspoon salt

2 large eggs

1 ¼ cups milk

½ teaspoon vanilla extract

3 tablespoons butter, plus more as needed

1. Preheat the oven to 200 degrees.
2. In a large bowl, whisk together the cornmeal, flour, sugar, baking powder, and salt. In a small bowl, combine eggs, milk, and vanilla. Pour the egg mixture into the dry ingredients and stir to combine. It's okay if the batter is a bit lumpy.
3. Heat the skillet over medium-high heat and melt some butter in it. When hot, make pancakes by spooning the batter into the pan. Cook for about 2 minutes on each side, until golden. Keep the pancakes warm on a plate in the oven. Serve with lots of butter.

If you have leftover corn on the cob, cut the kernels off of one, break them apart, and add them to the batter before cooking. They'll add texture, flavor, and some moisture. Consider serving with a sweet-spicy salsa, like one that has peaches in it.

SAUSAGE AND APPLE PIE

SERVES 4 TO 6 ✦ ACTIVE TIME: 30 MINUTES ✦ START TO FINISH: 60 MINUTES

If you know company is coming for the weekend and you want to be able to stay up late but still have something delicious and filling to serve in the morning, make this a day or two ahead of time and store it in the fridge, tightly covered. Then just take it out, let it come to room temperature while you preheat the oven and make the coffee, and bake it.

8 eggs

3 cups milk

1 teaspoon salt

1 teaspoon freshly ground pepper

1 cup grated mozzarella cheese

1 small loaf of raisin bread cut into small pieces

1 pound sweet Italian sausage, casing removed

2 tablespoons butter

1 small onion, diced

1 large Granny Smith apple, peeled, cored, and diced

3 tablespoons sugar

1 teaspoon dried sage

1 teaspoon red pepper flakes

1. Preheat the oven to 350 degrees.
2. In a large bowl, whisk together the eggs, milk, salt, and pepper. Stir in the cheese and bread, combining so that the bread absorbs the liquid.
3. Heat the skillet over medium-high heat and add the sausage, stirring to break up the meat and cook. Cook, stirring, until the sausage is cooked through. Transfer the cooked sausage to a plate or bowl with a slotted spoon. Add the onion and apple to the pan and cook, stirring, until the onion is translucent and the apple softens, about 5 minutes. Stir in the sugar, sage, and red pepper flakes.
4. Turn off the heat, and add the sausage, then the egg/bread mixture. Cover the skillet and bake in the oven for 30 minutes. Remove the cover and continue to cook for another 15 minutes until a knife inserted in the middle comes out clean. Remove from the oven and allow to cool slightly before serving.

For a really decadent addition to this dish, serve with warmed maple syrup to drizzle over the pie!

CORNED BEEF HASH

SERVES 4 TO 6 ✦ ACTIVE TIME: 40 MINUTES ✦ START TO FINISH: 90 MINUTES

If you like to eat this at a diner, wait until you make it yourself. It's so good!

2 large russet potatoes, peeled and cut into cubes

1 teaspoon salt

3 tablespoons butter

1 Vidalia onion, diced

3 cloves garlic, minced

1 red bell pepper, cored and seeded, chopped fine

1 pound corned beef, cut into bite-sized pieces

½ teaspoon dried thyme

Salt and freshly ground pepper to taste

1. Put the potatoes in a sauce pan and cover with cold water. Add the salt. Bring the water to a boil, then lower the heat and cook the potatoes about 10 minutes until partially cooked. (Cooking until soft will cause them to fall apart in the hash.) Drain them in a colander and rinse with cold water. Set aside.
2. Heat the butter in the skillet over medium-high heat. Add the onions, garlic, and pepper and cook, stirring, until the vegetables soften, about 3 minutes.
3. Add the potatoes and press them down into the skillet around the vegetables. Allow them to set and cook for about 5 minutes, then start turning sections over with a spatula while stirring in the corned beef. Sprinkle with the thyme, and season with salt and pepper. Continue to cook for about 5 minutes so that the potatoes are browned and the corned beef is warmed through. Season with additional salt and pepper if desired.

If you like eggs with your corned beef hash, once the potatoes are browned, make 4 to 6 indentations in the top of the hash and break the eggs into them. Lower the heat and cover the skillet. Continue cooking until the eggs are set, about 3 minutes.

BARBEQUED CHICKEN HASH

SERVES 4 TO 6 ✦ ACTIVE TIME: 40 MINUTES ✦ START TO FINISH: 90 MINUTES

Got some leftover barbequed chicken? Serve up a Tex-Mex breakfast with this flavorful hash.

2 large russet potatoes, peeled and cut into cubes

1 teaspoon salt

3 tablespoons butter

1 Vidalia onion, diced

3 cloves garlic, minced

1 small jalapeno pepper, cored and seeded, sliced

1 pound cooked barbequed chicken, cut into bite-sized pieces

¼ cup barbeque sauce

Salt and freshly ground pepper to taste

Salsa, sour cream, and sliced black olives to serve on the side

1. Put the potatoes in a sauce pan and cover with cold water. Add the salt. Bring the water to a boil, then lower the heat and cook the potatoes about 10 minutes until partially cooked. (Cooking until soft will cause them to fall apart in the hash.) Drain them in a colander and rinse with cold water. Set aside.
2. Heat the butter in the skillet over medium-high heat. Add the onions, garlic, and slices of jalapeno, and cook, stirring, until the vegetables soften, about 3 minutes.
3. Add the potatoes and press them down into the skillet around the vegetables. Allow them to set and cook for about 5 minutes, then start turning sections over with a spatula while stirring in the chicken and the barbeque sauce. Continue to cook for about 5 minutes so that the potatoes are browned and the meat is warmed through. Season with salt and pepper, and serve with sides of salsa, sour cream, and sliced black olives.

If you don't want to make this too hot, substitute a green bell pepper for the jalapeno pepper. People who like spicy can always add a favorite hot sauce to their serving.

ALMOND COFFEE CAKE

SERVES 6 TO 8 ✦ ACTIVE TIME: 90 MINUTES ✦ START TO FINISH: 2 HOURS

Toasted almonds and almond extract impart a heavenly taste and fragrance to this traditional morning cake.

Cake

1¾ cup flour

⅔ cup sugar

½ teaspoon baking soda

¼ teaspoon salt

8 tablespoons butter, softened

2 eggs

1 teaspoon almond extract

½ cup buttermilk

Topping

½ cup sugar

½ cup dark brown sugar

½ teaspoon ginger

¼ teaspoon salt

12 tablespoons (1½ sticks) unsalted butter, melted

2 cups flour

½ cup dried organic coconut

1. Preheat the oven to 325 degrees.
2. To make the cake, whisk together the flour, sugar, baking soda, and salt in a large bowl. Add the butter and stir with an electric mixer until blended.
3. In a small bowl, whisk together the eggs, almond extract, and buttermilk. Pour into the flour mixture and blend on high speed until the batter is light and fluffy. Pour the batter into a greased skillet.
4. To make the topping, whisk together the sugars, ginger, and salt in a bowl. Add the melted butter and combine. Then add the flour and coconut and stir to form a crumbly dough.
5. Dot the topping over the cake in the skillet. Put the skillet in the oven and bake for 45 minutes, until knife inserted in the middle comes out clean. Allow to cool for about 10 minutes before serving.

Fresh fruit is a great addition to this coffeecake. Before putting on the topping, sprinkle in some peeled, chopped pears, or some blueberries, or pears and cranberries.

HUEVOS RANCHEROS

SERVES 4 ✦ ACTIVE TIME: 25 MINUTES ✦ START TO FINISH: 40 MINUTES

Pretend you're in Mexico for the morning by serving this delicious—and filling—meal.

2 tablespoons vegetable oil

Four 6-inch corn tortillas

8 oz. refried beans

1 teaspoon butter

4 eggs

½ cup grated sharp cheddar cheese

½ cup grated Monterey Jack cheese

½ cup fresh salsa

Sliced jalapeno peppers (optional)

1. Heat oil in a skillet over medium-high heat. Fry the tortillas, one at a time, until firm but not crisp. Transfer cooked tortillas to a plate lined with a paper towel, and separate with paper towels while cooking.
2. Put the refried beans and butter in a bowl and heat in the microwave for about 1 minute, stirring halfway through.
3. Fry the eggs in the skillet over easy and sprinkle with cheese when nearly cooked so that cheese melts.
4. Prepare the dish by placing a tortilla on a plate, topping with the beans, then the egg and cheese. Serve hot with salsa and jalapenos on the side.

You can make this a one-dish meal. Cut the tortillas into 1/2-inch pieces and fry them, stirring. When crisped, spoon the refried beans and butter over them, pressing it into the bottom of the skillet to brown. Break the eggs over the beans and cover so that the eggs start to set. Cook for about 2 minutes. Take off the lid and cover with cheese. Take the skillet off the heat, cover so that the cheese melts completely, and serve.

MAPLE FRENCH TOAST

SERVES 4 ✦ ACTIVE TIME: 20 MINUTES ✦ START TO FINISH: 40 MINUTES

What better to do with leftover crusty bread than to soak it in some fresh eggs and cream, sizzle it up in some butter, and drizzle it with maple syrup? Enjoy it with strong coffee and thick-sliced bacon, that's what!

4 eggs

½ cup heavy cream

¾ cup all-natural maple syrup

8 slices slightly stale, thick-cut bread

4 tablespoons butter

1. Preheat the oven to 200 degrees and place an oven-proof serving dish in it.
2. In a small bowl, combine the eggs, heavy cream, and ½ cup of the maple syrup. Whisk to thoroughly combine, or use an immersion blender.
3. Put pieces of bread in a 13x9-inch baking dish and cover with the egg mixture. Let the bread soak up the egg mixture for about 20 minutes, turning halfway so both sides can soak.
4. Heat a 12-inch skillet over medium heat. Add 2 tablespoons of the butter and as it melts, tilt the pan to coat it evenly. When the butter is heated but not browned, add 4 slices of the soaked bread. Allow to cook for about 4 minutes, then flip them. Drizzle the pieces with maple syrup while they're cooking on the other side, and after another 4 minutes or so, flip them again so the side with the maple syrup gets cooked for a minute or so.
5. Transfer the cooked pieces to the serving dish in the oven. Repeat the cooking process for the remaining slices of bread.
6. Before serving, warm the maple syrup (and some additional syrup) in a microwave-safe container for 30 seconds. Test the warmth. You don't want to over-warm it, just take the chill out. Serve the French toast with maple syrup.

Many kinds of bread can be used to make French toast, from simple sandwich bread to hearty whole-grain loaves. The thicker the bread, the longer you should let it soak (up to overnight if desired). I like using country breads from a bakery that I can slice at home, especially when adding some maple syrup to the eggs and cream, which adds some sweetness. The sugar in the maple syrup will also caramelize on the skillet, which is great as long as it the heat is kept on medium, so it won't burn the sugar but simply "toast" it.

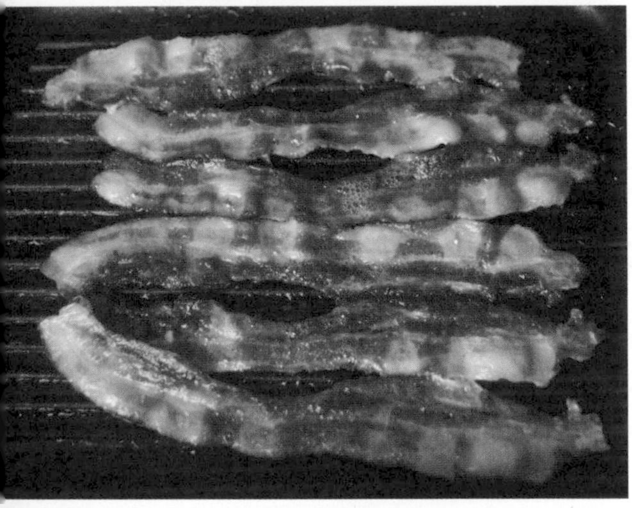

MAIN DISHES

When you're looking for something that's loaded with flavor to be the centerpiece of your meal, start in this chapter. The cast-iron skillet's versatility and practicality shine through when used to cook meats, fish, and casseroles. You'll find everything here from amazing salmon cakes to simple meat-and-veggie-stuffed pot pies and satisfyingly rich risottos. The cast-iron skillet does an amazing job of browning on the outside while retaining moisture on the inside. It can go from stove to oven and handle the heat from both, which means there are fewer pans and dishes to fuss with when you're preparing a main course. And so, without further ado, here are some recipes to whet your appetite and excite your senses.

BEST. BURGERS. EVER.

MAKES 4 TO 6 BURGERS ✦ ACTIVE TIME: 30 MINUTES ✦ START TO FINISH: 30 MINUTES

I won't argue that a burger hot off the grill is a delicious thing. It's a staple of American dining. But if you want the Best. Burger. Ever., you won't produce it on the grill. You'll make it in a cast iron skillet. Period. Why? Because the fat in the meat creates its own sauce, helping to brown and flavor the meat as it cooks. All of this drips off the grill. The cast iron holds the heat steady and hot, too, turning the surface of the burger the perfect crispy dark brown from side to side. If your mouth is watering now, wait until you make this at home.

1 pound ground beef

Salt and pepper for seasoning

Hamburger buns (not too bready)

Slices of cheese (optional)

Lettuce, tomato, and onion (optional)

Ketchup, mustard, pickles, mayonnaise (optional)

1. Refrigerate the hamburger meat until ready to use.
2. When it's time to make the burgers, first brush your skillet with a thin sheen of oil, and heat it over medium-high heat. Take the meat out of the fridge and form the patties. Don't overhandle the meat, simply take a handful of it (about 3 oz.), and gently form into a patty. Make 3 or 4, depending on how many will fit in the skillet.
3. Put the patties in the skillet and don't touch them. Let them start to cook on the medium-high heat. They'll spatter and sizzle. That's fine. Sprinkle some salt on them, and grind some pepper over them (but not too much). Let them cook on one side for about 3 minutes.
4. When you flip the burgers, if you want cheese on one or all of them, put it on now. The cheese should blanket the meat, not be an afterthought.
5. Leave the burgers to cook on this side just as you did the other side. The skillet takes care of even distribution of the heat. Wait 3 or 4 minutes. Scoop the burger off the skillet with the spatula, slide it onto a bun, top with whatever you like, and dig in. Best. Burgers. Ever.

The kind of meat you use matters. The meat-to-fat ratio should be about 80-20. Most ground beef found in the grocery store is 85-15 or 90-10. If you have to go with one of these, choose the fattier proportion. The best thing to do, though, is ask the meat department to grind the meat for you. You want a chuck cut with a good amount of fat in it. The fat should show up as almost chunky in the meat, not pulverized into the grind to look like pale red mush. Trust me on this one.

STEAK FRITES

SERVES 2 ✦ ACTIVE TIME: 30 MINUTES ✦ START TO FINISH: 2 HOURS

A hot, juicy steak… yummy. A mound of hot, crispy French fries… fabulous! Now combine them, and you'll understand why the French have this dish on the menu of nearly every bistro in the country. And you can create them both in your skillet.

For the Fries

1 pound Yukon gold potatoes, peeled, washed, and cut into thin strips

3 cups peanut oil (Although increasingly difficult to find, peanut is the best oil to fry in. If you can't find it, vegetable oil is a suitable substitute.)

Salt and pepper to taste

For the Steak

2 small steaks (best is sirloin, rib eye, or shell), about 1 inch thick

3 tablespoons unsalted butter

Salt and pepper to taste

Fresh parsley for garnish

1. Preheat the oven to 200 degrees.
2. Prepare everything ahead of time so you can cook the steaks immediately after the fries. If you wait too long, the fries will get soft. Line a baking sheet with paper towels (for the fries when they're cooked). Put the steaks on a plate in the refrigerator (keep them cold until ready for to go in the pan). Make sure your potato strips are clean and dry.
3. Put the oil in the skillet and add the potatoes. Bring the oil to a boil over medium-high heat (careful of splattering). As the oil gets hotter, the potatoes will get limp and just start to brown (about 15 minutes). At this point, start turning them with tongs to get all sides crispy and browned. Cook another 5 minutes or so.
4. Transfer the fries to the baking sheet and sprinkle with salt. Put in the oven to stay warm, covering with additional paper towels so they stay crisp.
5. Drain the fat from the skillet into a heat-proof glass container (like a measuring cup). Put the skillet back on the burner and add the butter. Take the steaks out of the fridge. When the butter is hot but not smoking, put the steaks in the skillet. Sear them over the high heat for a minute per side, then reduce the heat to medium. Sprinkle with salt and pepper and turn them every few minutes. They're cooked in about 8 minutes (so that they're somewhat rare and juicy inside).
6. Transfer to plates, and pile the French fries next to them. Garnish with parsley. *Voila!*

STEAK AU POIVRE

SERVES 2 ACTIVE TIME: 40 MINUTES START TO FINISH: 2 HOURS

After making the Steak Frites (page 69), the natural progression was to experiment and create the other classic French bistro fare, steak au poivre *(with pepper). You'll get the best results if you use the best ingredients: farm-fresh for the meat, shallots, chives, and cream, if at all possible.* Bon appetite!

2 boneless strip steaks (about 8 oz. each)

Kosher salt

1 tablespoon whole black peppercorns

1 teaspoon vegetable oil

2 small shallots, minced

2 tablespoons unsalted butter, cut into pieces

⅓ cup cognac or other brandy

½ cup heavy cream

Preheat oven to 200 degrees.

Prep steaks by patting dry, then seasoning both sides with kosher salt.

Put the peppercorns in a sealed plastic bag and working on a hard, flat surface, pound them with a meat tenderizer or mallet to coarsely crush them. Pour them onto a plate and press both sides of both steaks into them, distributing peppercorns evenly on the meat.

Heat the skillet over medium-high heat until hot. Add the oil, coating the bottom of the pan. Put the steaks on the pan and sear on both sides, cooking for about 3 minutes a side for medium-rare.

Transfer steaks to a platter in the oven and keep warm as you make the sauce.

With the skillet on medium heat, add a tablespoon of the butter, let it melt, and add shallots. As they saute, stir up the bits stuck to the bottom of the pan. Cook until shallots are browned, about 3 minutes. Pour the cognac in the pan, swirl it around, and using a long-handled lighter, ignite it. The flame will subside in a minute or so. Continue to cook sauce until it is nearly boiling, stirring constantly.

Add the cream and any juices from the platter the steaks are on. Reduce the heat and cook the sauce until somewhat reduced, about 5 minutes. Stir in the last tablespoon of butter.

Put the steaks on a plate and pour the sauce over them. Garnish with rosemary, if desired.

SALMON CAKES

MAKES 6 TO 8 CAKES ✦ ACTIVE TIME: 60 MINUTES ✦ START TO FINISH: 90 MINUTES

I use canned salmon for this recipe. The quality isn't as high as using freshly steamed salmon, but it's quite good. With the healthy add-ins, and the fact that the end product is a cake that will be topped with a dressing like tartar or cocktail sauce, the canned salmon is great for ease of use and taste.

2 (14.75-oz.) cans of salmon (preferably Red Salmon over Pink Salmon)

2 large eggs, lightly beaten

4 tablespoons bread crumbs

¼ cup onion, minced

1 teaspoon Frank's Red Hot sauce

1 teaspoon dried parsley flakes

Salt and freshly ground pepper to taste

2 tablespoons oil (preferably peanut, but olive is fine)

Lemon wedges

1. Drain the liquid from the cans of salmon, and empty the fish into a bowl, flaking it apart with a fork. Add the eggs, bread crumbs, minced onion, hot sauce, and parsley flakes and stir, combining well. Season with salt and pepper.
2. Heat the skillet over medium-high heat. Add 1 tablespoon of the oil. Add 3 or 4 individual heaping spoons full of fish mix to the skillet, pressing down on the tops of each to form a patty (cake). Brown the cakes on each side for about 5 minutes. Try to turn the cakes over just once. If you're worried about them being cooked through, put a lid on the skillet for a minute or so after they've browned on each side.
3. Transfer the cakes to a plate and cover with foil to keep them warm while you cook the next batch. Serve on a platter with lemon wedges.

Variations

Salmon cakes can be served many ways:

- Eat them as you would hamburgers, on a bun with lettuce, tomato, red onion, and instead of ketchup or mustard, tartar or cocktail sauce.
- Serve a cake on top of a green salad with a lemon-dill dressing on the side.
- Make mini cakes and serve as finger foods with toothpicks and dipping sauces.

SIMPLY SENSATIONAL CHILI CON CARNE

SERVES 4 TO 6 ✦ ACTIVE TIME: 20 MINUTES ✦ START TO FINISH: 40 MINUTES

Chili is another dish that has as many variations as people who like to cook and eat it. This one is basic and elemental so that, if you want, you can embellish it to your liking with spicier or more exotic seasonings, different cuts of meat, and so on.

Vegetable oil

½ onion, diced

1 pound ground beef

1 (15.5-oz.) can kidney beans, drained and rinsed

1 (15.5-oz.) can diced tomatoes, with juice

3 oz. (½ can) tomato paste

⅓ cup chili powder

1 tablespoon garlic powder

1 teaspoon cumin

½ teaspoon oregano

1 teaspoon cayenne pepper

Salt and pepper to taste

1. Heat the skillet over medium-high heat. Add scant teaspoon vegetable oil to just coat the pan, and add the onion, stirring to cook, until translucent, about 2 minutes. Add the ground meat, breaking it up as you stir to cook it. Brown the meat so that it's cooked through, about 10 minutes.
2. Drain the meat over a colander in the sink to remove fat. Put the meat back in the skillet.
3. Over medium heat, stir in the beans, tomatoes, tomato paste, chili powder, garlic powder, cumin, oregano, and cayenne. Combine thoroughly and bring the mix to a slow boil. Season with salt and pepper. Continue to cook on low for 10 to 15 minutes. Serve hot in bowls.

Corn chips are one of my guilty pleasures, so I always take the opportunity to garnish my chili with crumbled corn chips (or I use them as scoops for the chili). At our table, we also put out bowls of shredded cheddar cheese, sour cream, jalapeno slices, and thinly sliced scallions. Some like to serve chili with rice, which is good, too.

BEEF BRISKET

SERVES 6 TO 8 ✦ ACTIVE TIME: 30 MINUTES ✦ START TO FINISH: 9 HOURS

Brisket is the name of the cut of meat from a cow that's taken from the breast. It is a tough piece of meat that needs a long, slow cooking time—but it's worth it, because the slow cooking tenderizes the meat and brings out the flavor. A little prep time, and the meat can cook in the skillet in the oven for a solid 8 hours, leaving you free to do other things.

8-pound brisket, with a layer of fat on it or with marbling of fat

1 teaspoon vegetable oil

Salt and pepper

1. Preheat the oven to 250 degrees.
2. Heat a large cast-iron skillet over medium-high heat. When it's hot, add the vegetable oil, then put the brisket in fat side down so it starts to cook. Sear the meat on both sides, about 3 minutes a side, and season with salt and pepper.
3. Put the skillet in the oven with the brisket facing fat side up. Cook for 8 hours, checking on it every few hours to be sure it isn't drying out, but this is unlikely.
4. Cook until the meat is very tender, falling apart with a fork.

Some serious BBQ competitions feature brisket, and different chefs have different "secret ingredients" to transform this cut. Some use barbeque rubs with everything from cayenne to cumin to special peppers. Some start the heat high and then lower it. If you want a flavored brisket, explore putting a rub together. You'll need to add it as you would the salt and pepper in this recipe. But I prefer to serve the basic brisket with different barbeque sauces on the side.

JUICY TURKEY BURGERS

SERVES 4 TO 6 ✦ ACTIVE TIME: 20 MINUTES ✦ START TO FINISH: 60 MINUTES

I love the idea of using ground turkey to reduce the fat in recipes where I'd normally use ground beef. Unfortunately, the taste is never the same, and it's for that very reason: less fat! It turns out that shredded zucchini can moisten—and flavor—ground turkey, making for a very satisfying (and low-fat) experience.

Olive oil

½ cup onion, diced fine

2 cloves garlic, pressed

¾ cup plain bread crumbs

1 teaspoon tamari (or soy sauce)

½ teaspoon fresh ground pepper

1 teaspoon salt

¼ teaspoon dried sage

1 tablespoon fresh parsley, chopped fine

½ cup zucchini, grated or shredded in a food processor

¼ cup grated mozzarella

1 pound ground turkey

Tzatziki sauce (page 19)

1. Heat the skillet over medium-high heat and coat with about a teaspoon of olive oil. Add the onions and garlic and cook, stirring, until the onion is translucent, about 3 minutes. Remove from heat and transfer the onion mix to a large bowl.
2. Add the bread crumbs, tamari, pepper, salt, sage, parsley, zucchini, and mozzarella. Combine well. Add the turkey and stir to mix the ingredients together.
3. Form the meat into patties and refrigerate, wrapped in plastic, for 30 minutes.
4. Heat the skillet over medium-high heat and add about a teaspoon of olive oil. Place the patties in the skillet and cook for about 4 minutes per side. Do not overflip or flatten the patties while cooking.
5. Because you want the turkey cooked through the center, reduce the heat to medium and cover the skillet. Continue to cook for another 3 to 4 minutes. Press down gently on one of the patties to see if the juice is running clear. If it's still pink, continue to cook another minute or so.
6. Season with additional salt and pepper, and serve on hamburger buns with toppings of your choice. I choose Tzatziki sauce (page 19).

CHICKEN FAJITAS

SERVES 6 TO 8 ✦ ACTIVE TIME: 30 MINUTES ✦ START TO FINISH: 5 HOURS

The trick is to bring this dish to the table while the meat and veggies are still sizzling. You'll want to be sure you have all the sides prepped ahead of time so you can go straight from stove to table with this. You'll want tortillas, guacamole, salsa, jalapenos, sliced black olives, and sour cream.

For the Chicken

½ cup orange juice

1 lime, squeezed (about 3 tablespoons juice)

4 cloves garlic, minced

1 jalapeno pepper, ribs and seeds removed, diced

2 tablespoons fresh cilantro, chopped

1 teaspoon cumin

1 teaspoon dried oregano

Salt and pepper

3 tablespoons olive oil

3 to 4 boneless, skinless chicken breasts, cut into strips

1. In a bowl, combine orange juice, lime juice, garlic, jalapeno, cilantro, cumin, oregano, and salt and pepper. When thoroughly combined, add the olive oil. Put the chicken pieces in the mix, stir, cover with plastic wrap and refrigerate for about 4 hours.
2. About an hour before you want to eat, get the sides prepared so you'll have them on hand when the dish is sizzling.
3. Heat the skillet over medium-high heat. Remove the chicken from the marinade with a slotted spoon and put it in the skillet, stirring and turning the pieces so they brown on all sides. Cook thoroughly, about 8 to 10 minutes. Transfer the cooked chicken to a platter and cover loosely with foil to keep warm.
4. Reduce the heat to medium, add the oil, and then add the onion, peppers, jalapeno, and garlic. Cook, stirring, for 3 to 5 minutes until vegetables soften. Add the lime juice and cilantro and cook for a few minutes more. Season with salt and pepper.
5. While vegetables are still sizzling, push them to one side of the pan and put the chicken on the other side. Serve immediately.

You can use the same ingredients to make steak fajitas, but substitute 1 pound of flank steak for the chicken, and marinate it in the mix overnight. Don't slice the steak until it has been cooked.

For the Vegetables

2 tablespoons olive oil

1 red onion, thinly sliced

1 red bell pepper, ribs and seeds removed, thinly sliced

1 green bell pepper, ribs and seeds removed, thinly sliced

1 yellow bell pepper, ribs and seeds removed, thinly sliced

2 jalapeno peppers or serrano chiles, ribs and seeds removed, sliced thin

3 cloves garlic, minced

¼ cup fresh-squeezed lime juice

½ cup fresh cilantro, chopped

Salt and pepper to taste

FRIED CHICKEN

SERVES 4 ✦ ACTIVE TIME: 60 MINUTES ✦ START TO FINISH: 90 MINUTES

If you want the texture and flavor of chicken fried in oil without the mess of the oil, try this recipe. The corn flakes are essential!

3 chicken legs (drums and thighs together, cut to make 3 drumsticks and 3 thighs)

¼ cup flour

Salt and pepper

1 cup milk

1 tablespoon white vinegar

2 eggs, lightly beaten

1½ cups corn flakes, finely crushed

½ cup plain breadcrumbs

1 teaspoon paprika

1 cup vegetable oil

1. Preheat the oven to 400 degrees. Place the skillet in the oven to get it hot.
2. Rinse and dry the chicken pieces.
3. In a shallow bowl or cake pan, whisk together the flour with some salt and pepper. In the measuring cup of milk, add the vinegar and let the combination sit for 10 minutes (to create buttermilk). When ready, mix the milk in a bowl with the beaten eggs. In another large bowl, combine the corn flakes, bread crumbs, paprika, and 2 tablespoons of the vegetable oil.
4. Coat the chicken pieces one at a time by dipping each in the flour, then the milk mixture, then the crumb mixture, being sure to coat all sides. When coated, put the pieces on a plate, cover with plastic wrap, and refrigerate for about 15 minutes.
5. Remembering how hot it's going to be (wear oven mitts!), take the skillet out of the oven and put the oil in it. Heat it on low until hot. Add the cold chicken pieces and turn in the hot oil so both sides are coated with oil.
6. Put the skillet back in the oven and bake for about 30 minutes, turning the pieces after 15 minutes. The chicken is done when the juices run clear when pierced with a knife. Serve immediately.

SEAFOOD PAELLA

SERVES 4 TO 6 ✦ ACTIVE TIME: 90 MINUTES ✦ START TO FINISH: 2 HOURS

Paella is a rice dish that hails from Valencia in Spain. Its yellow hue comes from saffron threads, and it is chock full of everything good: rice, meat, fish, and vegetables. This recipe is made with more seafood than meat, and it's for a smaller serving size than a platter that would normally feed a party.

4 cups chicken broth

2 tablespoons olive oil, as needed

1 onion, diced

4 cloves garlic, minced

1 teaspoon smoked paprika

½ teaspoon saffron threads, crushed

2½ cups short-grain rice (Arborio or paella)

2 ripe tomatoes, seeded and chopped

1 cup dry white wine

1 teaspoon salt

Freshly ground black pepper

1 cup frozen peas

½ pound calamari, cut into 1-inch pieces

8 oz. Spanish chorizo, cut into ¼-inch rounds

½ pound small shrimp, peeled and deveined

16 mussels, scrubbed and debearded

1. Preheat the oven to 425 degrees.
2. In a saucepan, bring the chicken broth to a simmer over medium heat.
3. Heat the skillet over medium- high heat. Add the olive oil, onion, and garlic, and cook, stirring occasionally, until the onion is translucent, about 3 minutes. Add the paprika and saffron, and cook, stirring, for another minute.
4. Add the rice, stirring to coat, then stir in the tomatoes and wine. Bring to a boil, cooking until the liquid is reduced by half, about 2 minutes. Add the hot chicken broth and peas, stir, then bring to a boil and cook for 5 minutes. Season with salt and pepper.
5. Add the peas, calamari, and chorizo and stir to combine. Put the skillet in the oven and bake for about 30 minutes, until the calamari are soft. Scatter the shrimp and mussels over the top of the paella and return to the oven. Cook until the shrimp are opaque and the mussels have opened, 5 to 10 minutes.
6. Keep an eye on the dish so the seafood on top doesn't overcook.
7. Remove from the oven, discard any mussel shells that didn't open, let rest for about 5 minutes, and serve.

CAST-IRON TIPS

Cast-iron
skillets can take
the heat more than
any other pan,
making them the
perfect tools for
searing meat.

CRAB CAKES

MAKES 6 CAKES **ACTIVE TIME: 60 MINUTES** **START TO FINISH: 90 MINUTES**

With these cakes, if you want great flavor, you have to go for top-quality crab meat. This is the kind that's in the refrigerated section of your store's fish department. Don't buy crab meat that's canned like tuna. It has neither the flavor nor the consistency needed for these cakes.

1 pound lump crab meat

¼ cup onion, minced

½ cup bread crumbs

1 teaspoon Worcestershire sauce

1 teaspoon Old Bay seasoning

1 teaspoon dried parsley flakes

1 tablespoon mayonnaise

1 tablespoons milk

1 large egg, lightly beaten

Salt and freshly ground pepper to taste

¼ cup oil (preferably peanut, but olive is fine)

Lemon wedges

In a large bowl combine crab meat, onion, bread crumbs, Worcestershire sauce, Old Bay seasoning, parsley flakes, and mayonnaise. Mix the milk into the egg and add to the crab mix, blending gently but thoroughly. Season with salt and pepper. If mix seems dry, add some more mayonnaise.

Heat the skillet over medium-high heat. Add the oil. It should be about ¼-inch deep. When oil is hot, add 3 or 4 individual heaping spoons full of crab mix to the skillet, pressing down on the tops of each to form a patty (cake). Brown the cakes on each side for about 3 minutes. Try to turn the cakes over just once. If you're worried about them being cooked through, put a lid on the skillet for a minute or so after they've browned on each side.

Transfer the cakes to a plate and cover with foil to keep them warm while you cook the next batch. Serve on a platter with lemon wedges.

Crabs in the Chesapeake Bay area of Maryland are served with Old Bay seasoning. The Old Bay Seasoning mix you purchase in a store is a proprietary blend, so the proportions aren't known for sure, but it's a combination of celery salt, paprika, cayenne, cloves, ginger, allspice, mustard, cinnamon, and more. The package says it's good on crabs, shrimp, and chicken—and those who love it agree. There's even a potato chip flavored with Old Bay.

CHICKEN-QUINOA CASSEROLE

SERVES 4 TO 6 ✦ ACTIVE TIME: 45 MINUTES ✦ START TO FINISH: 90 MINUTES

Using frozen vegetables in this recipe is a real time-saver. The turmeric adds a delicate spiciness, too.

1 tablespoon olive oil

½ onion, diced

2 cloves garlic, minced

1 pound boneless, skinless chicken breast, cut into 1-inch pieces

½ cup frozen vegetables (peas, beans, carrots, corn)

1 teaspoon turmeric

½ teaspoon salt

½ teaspoon black pepper

12 oz. crushed tomatoes or chopped tomatoes in puree

1 cup water

1 cup uncooked quinoa

¼ cup chopped parsley

½ cup crumbled feta cheese

1. Heat the skillet over medium-high heat. Add the olive oil, onion, and garlic and cook for 2 minutes or until translucent.
2. Add the chicken pieces and frozen vegetables and continue to cook, stirring, until chicken pieces are browned, about 8 minutes. Stir in the turmeric and season with salt and pepper.
3. Add the tomatoes and water, and bring to a boil. Stir in the quinoa, reduce the heat to medium, and cook for 15 to 20 minutes until quinoa is cooked and a lot of the liquid has evaporated. Stir in the parsley and sprinkle with feta cheese. Serve.

Quinoa is a "super food" that has been a part of the human diet for several thousand years, since the Incas deemed it fit for human consumption. It is a seed that is prepared like a grain. It contains all nine amino acids and is rich in lysine, iron, magnesium, and riboflavin. Quinoa also has more fiber than grains. On its own, its flavor is somewhat nuttier than brown rice and its texture is grainier. It is a great base upon which to add vegetables and grilled meat or fish.

LAMB CHOPS WITH ROSEMARY AND LEMON

SERVES 4 ✦ ACTIVE TIME: 15 MINUTES ✦ START TO FINISH: 30 MINUTES

Lamb chops are an indulgence, for sure, so if you're going to splurge, be sure to follow this recipe when preparing them. The rosemary, garlic, and lemon seasoning bring out the earthy goodness of the chops to perfection.

4 tablespoons fresh-squeezed lemon juice (no seeds)

2 tablespoons fresh rosemary leaves, chopped

2 cloves garlic, pressed

Salt and pepper to taste

8 lamb chops

1. Preheat the broiler on high. Position a rack to be about 5 to 7 inches away from the heat. Put the skillet in the oven so it gets hot.
2. In a bowl, combine the lemon juice and rosemary. Press the garlic into the mix and season with salt and pepper. Using your hands, rub the chops in the mix, being sure to coat both sides and distribute evenly. Put the chops on a platter.
3. When the skillet is hot, take it out and position the chops in it so they fit. Return to the rack under the broiler and cook for about 5 minutes. Since the skillet is already hot, the lamb is cooking on both sides at once.
4. Remove from the oven, let rest for a minute, and serve.

LIVER AND ONIONS

SERVES 4 TO 6 ✦ ACTIVE TIME: 40 MINUTES ✦ START TO FINISH: 7 HOURS

My family thinks I'm crazy because I get very excited when I see a beautiful piece of calf's liver. I can smell and practically taste its pungent, buttery goodness, slathered with sautéed onions. My mother used to make it for my family as a treat, and it was delicious every time. Serve this with homemade mashed potatoes, which are the perfect food to soak up the oil and butter from the liver and onions. And if you want to be completely decadent, serve creamed spinach, too.

1 pound calf's liver (not beef liver, which is not as tender)

1½ cups milk

3 tablespoons butter

2 onions, thinly sliced (not diced)

½ cup flour

Salt and freshly ground pepper

2 tablespoons butter

Chopped fresh parsley for garnish

1. To prep the liver, put it in a glass bowl and cover with the milk. Cover the bowl with plastic wrap, and refrigerate the meat for 5 to 6 hours.
2. Heat skillet over medium heat. Add the butter. When butter is melted, add onion slices. Stir to separate and coat with the butter. Cook over medium heat just until onions begin to soften, about 6 minutes. Reduce the heat to low and cook, stirring occasionally for 30 to 40 minutes.
3. While the onions are cooking, remove the liver from the milk. Cut into 2 pieces and pat dry with paper towels. Put the flour on a plate and season with salt and pepper. Gently press the liver pieces into the flour to coat them. Shake off excess.
4. Heat another cast-iron or heavy-bottomed skillet over medium heat. Add the remaining butter. When hot but not browned, add the liver pieces. Saute the pieces for about 2 to 3 minutes a side so that they are browned on the outside but slightly pink inside. Be careful not to overcook them.
5. When done, transfer to a plate and pile on the sautéed onions. Sprinkle the chopped fresh parsley over the plate and serve.

Calf liver is milder than beef liver. Even so, soaking liver in milk is a way to remove any bitter flavor.

MOUSSAKA

SERVES 4 TO 6 ✦ ACTIVE TIME: 90 MINUTES ✦ START TO FINISH: 2 HOURS

This Greek dish is an incredible blend of lamb, eggplant, and spices. Topped with a cheesy crust, this is a great alternative to shepherd's pie.

For the Filling

1 large eggplant, end trimmed and cut into cubes

¼ cup salt

4 cups cold water

⅓ cup olive oil

1 pound ground lamb

1 onion, diced

3 cloves garlic, minced

½ cup dry red wine

8-oz. can tomato sauce

2 tablespoons fresh parsley, chopped

1 teaspoon dried oregano

½ teaspoon cinnamon

Salt and pepper to taste

For the Crust

5 eggs

6 tablespoons butter

⅓ cup flour

2½ cups milk

⅔ cup grated Parmesan cheese

⅓ cup fresh dill, chopped (or substitute parsley)

1. Preheat the oven to 350 degrees.
2. Prep the eggplant by putting the cold water in a bowl and adding the salt. When dissolved, add the eggplant cubes and stir. Cover the bowl with plastic wrap and let the cubes soak for about 20 minutes. After soaking, drain the water off in a colander and rinse with cold water. Squeeze the cubes in your hands to wring out the water, place them on a pile of paper towels, and blot them as dry as possible. Set aside.
3. While the eggplant is soaking, heat the skillet over medium-high heat. Add a tablespoon of oil to coat the bottom. Brown the ground lamb in the skillet until cooked, about 4 minutes. Use a slotted spoon to transfer the cooked meat to a bowl. Set aside.
4. Cook the prepared eggplant. Heat the skillet over medium-high heat again. Add ¼ cup of olive oil and add the cubes, stirring frequently, until they start to soften, about 5 minutes. Use the slotted spoon to add the cooked eggplant to the bowl with the lamb in it.
5. Put the skillet back on the heat and add the rest of the oil. Cook the onion and garlic together, stirring constantly, until the onion is translucent, about 3 minutes. Add the lamb and eggplant and stir to combine. Add the wine, tomato sauce, parsley, oregano, and cinnamon. Stir to combine, lower the heat to low, and cook, simmering, for about 15 minutes, stirring occasionally. Season with salt and pepper.
6. Next, make the topping. In a large bowl, beat the eggs lightly. Heat another skillet or saucepan over medium heat, melt the butter, lower the heat slightly, and add the flour, stirring to combine and form a paste. Slowly add the milk, stirring with a whisk. Bring to a boil over low heat, stirring constantly with the whisk. When the mixture reaches a boil, remove from the heat. Add about half the hot mix into the eggs and stir briskly, then pour the tempered eggs into the skillet and mix into the rest of the hot flour/milk mix. Add the cheese and dill (or parsley) and stir.
7. Smooth the topping over the lamb in the first skillet to even it out, then top with the flour/cheese mix. Put the skillet in the oven. Bake for 35 to 45 minutes until the topping is set and golden brown.
8. Allow to rest for about 5 minutes before serving.

GRILLED PORK CHOPS WITH SUCCOTASH

MAKES 4 TO 6 SERVINGS ✦ ACTIVE TIME: 1 HOUR AND 20 MINUTES ✦ START TO FINISH: 2 HOURS

Pork is the perfect accompaniment to vegetables, and the lovely glaze created in the skillet adds another element of deliciousness. Using a cast-iron skillet on the grill adds a unique flavor to your dish.

For the Pork Chops

4 to 5 boneless pork chops, about 2 inches thick

2 tablespoons clarified butter

3 tablespoons of olive oil

¾ cup of red wine

Salt and pepper, to taste

For the Succotash

1 cup corn, canned or cut fresh from ears

1 cup pinto beans, or other preferred type of bean

1 cup green beans, cut into 1 inch pieces

1 cup carrots, cut into bite-sized pieces

2 tablespoons olive oil

1 tablespoon butter, cut into pieces

Salt and pepper to taste

Watercress for garnish

1. Get your grill started, aiming for a temperature of about 375 to 400 degrees.
2. Melt the clarified butter and olive oil in the cast-iron skillet. Add the pork chops and cook over the grill until evenly browned.
3. When the pork chops are nearly finished browning, add the wine to cook off the alcohol and to reduce the wine so it becomes a nice, flavorful stock. Add salt and pepper to your preferred taste.
4. Grill the pork chops over the open flame to sear in the final flavors, about 2-3 minutes per side. As the chops have already cooked in the saucepan, they should not need more long on each side before being ready to serve. We always try to let our meats and chops stand for about 10 minutes before serving.
5. While the pork chops are resting, prepare the succotash. Heat the oil in the skillet over medium-high heat on a stovetop or over the grill. Add the green beans and carrots and sauté for about 2 minutes. Add the pinto beans and corn and sauté for another 4-5 minutes, or until vegetables are tender. Mix in the butter, salt, and pepper. Garnish with watercress and serve with pork chops.

SUPER-EASY SPARERIBS

SERVES 2 TO 4 ✦ ACTIVE TIME: 2 HOURS ✦ START TO FINISH: 2 HOURS

Oven roasting in a skillet renders tender ribs with no hassle. Make these on a cold winter night, and you can pretend you're at a summertime picnic.

2 pounds pork spareribs

Salt and pepper for seasoning

Juice from ½ lemon

1 to 2 cups barbeque sauce

1. Preheat the oven to 350 degrees.
2. Wash and dry the ribs, cutting into sections that will fit in the skillet. Season both sides with salt and pepper.
3. Put the ribs in the skillet, sprinkle with fresh-squeezed lemon juice, and put the skillet in the oven. Bake for about 90 minutes, turning halfway through cooking time.
4. For the second half of the cooking time, brush with barbeque sauce, if desired, and turn again for the last 15 minutes, putting barbeque sauce on the other side of the ribs. Serve immediately.

PORK STUFFED WITH PRUNES

SERVES 4 TO 6 ✦ ACTIVE TIME: 60 MINUTES ✦ START TO FINISH: 2 HOURS

Prunes are dried plums, just like raisins are dried grapes. They're associated with the diets of elderly people, which is unfortunate, because they're quite tasty cooked or eaten in combination with other foods. Try this dish on your family without telling them what it is. You'll be pleasantly surprised—it's delicious!

8 pitted prunes

1 pound pork tenderloin, 2 to 3 pounds

2 cloves garlic, cut into thin sliversKitchen string

½ teaspoon ground ginger

1½ teaspoons kosher salt

½ teaspoon freshly ground pepper

3 tablespoons butter

1 cup water

½ cup dry white wine

1 tablespoon cornstarch or arrowroot

1. Preheat oven to 325 degrees.
2. In a small bowl, soak the prunes in hot water for about 15 minutes. Drain and dry with paper towels.
3. Cut the tenderloin open length-wise but not all the way through—like a pocket. Using the tip of a sharp knife, make some incisions and insert the garlic slivers.
4. Lay the soaked prunes across the meat and fold the other half of the meat over them. Tie the roast together with pieces of kitchen string. Season all over with the ginger, salt, and pepper.
5. Heat the skillet over medium-high heat. Add the butter. When it's melted, place the roast in it and allow to sear, turning so all sides are done, about 2 minutes per side. Add the water and wine to the pan and transfer the skillet to the oven. Roast, uncovered, for 1 hour, basting with pan juices every 20 minutes or so. Remove skillet from oven and transfer roast to a serving platter.
6. Meanwhile, make gravy by heating the juices in the pan over medium-high heat. In a small bowl, whisk together the cornstarch with 2 tablespoons water until blended. Add to the hot juices and stir in completely so there are no lumps. Cook, stirring, until gravy is smooth and thick. Pour over the roast before slicing, or serve on the side.

STUFFED PORK CHOPS

SERVES 4 ✦ ACTIVE TIME: 60 MINUTES ✦ START TO FINISH: 90 MINUTES

When cool temperatures have you thinking about ways to roast meats with dried fruits and nuts, this recipe will appeal to everything you're craving.

4 boneless pork chops

Salt and pepper

2 tablespoons olive oil

½ onion, minced

1 cup bread pieces from a thick, crusty bread like a baguette or sourdough loaf

½ cup dates, pitted and chopped

¼ cup walnuts, coarsely chopped

2 tablespoons port wine

2 tablespoons fresh sage, chopped

2 cups chicken broth

½ cup dry white wine

1. Preheat the oven to 400 degrees.
2. Rinse and pat dry the pork chops. Using a long, sharp knife, cut an incision into the meat to form a pocket. Season the chops with salt and pepper all over.
3. Heat the skillet over medium-high heat. Add the olive oil and onion and cook, stirring, until onion is soft, about 3 minutes. Reduce the heat to medium and add the bread cubes, dates, walnuts, port wine, and sage, stirring gently to combine. Cook for a couple of minutes until well blended. Remove pan from the heat.
4. Fill the pockets of the chops with the stuffing. Brush the skillet with oil, put it over medium-high heat, and add the chops, searing on both sides for about 3 minutes a side. Add the chicken broth and wine. Put the skillet in the oven and roast for about 20 minutes or until pork is cooked through. Baste with the pan juices after about 10 minutes. Let the chops rest for about 5 minutes before serving.

SPICY SAUSAGE STEW WITH SUMMER VEGETABLES

SERVES 4 TO 6 ✦ ACTIVE TIME: 35 MINUTES ✦ START TO FINISH: 60 MINUTES

When everything looks so good at the farmer's markets in the late summer, it's easy to end up at home with a lot of vegetables and few ideas of how to combine them to make something just right. This dish showcases the flavors of peppers, corn, and tomatoes, with just the right amount of spice.

2 tablespoons butter

1 onion, diced

2 cloves garlic, minced

1 pound Italian sausage, cut into slices

2 teaspoons chili powder

½ teaspoon cayenne pepper

2 red peppers, diced

3 ears of corn, shucked and cleaned, kernels removed

1 small zucchini, cut into half-moon slices about ¼ inch thick

4 tomatoes, seeds removed, cut into chunks

Salt and pepper

1. Heat the skillet over medium-high heat. Add the butter. When it is melted, add the onions and garlic and cook, stirring, until translucent and slightly browned, about 5 minutes.
2. Add the meat and stir, browning on all sides, about 3 minutes. Stir in the spices. Top with the peppers, corn, zucchini, and tomato pieces. Stir and season with salt and pepper.
3. Cover the skillet, reduce the heat to medium, and cook, covered, for about 20 minutes, checking it occasionally to be sure there is enough liquid and that it's at a gentle simmer, not a rolling boil. Garnish with parsley if desired. Serve immediately.

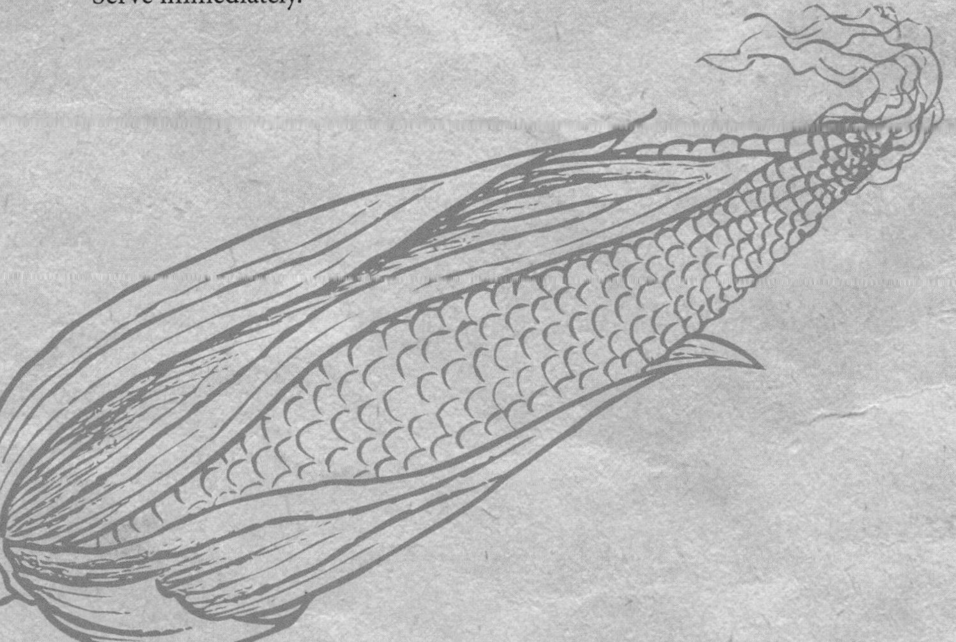

BEEF STROGANOFF

SERVES 4 TO 6 ✦ ACTIVE TIME: 40 MINUTES ✦ START TO FINISH: 90 MINUTES

The history of this dish in my house is that it was a favorite of my family's when I was growing up, so I made it for mine as they were growing up. I'm happy to say that they've liked mine as much as I liked my mother's. But the dish itself is Russian (Stroganov), made with pieces of beef served in a rich sauce that includes sour cream (Smetana). It purportedly became popular in the mid-1800s.

1 tablespoon olive oil

1 pound beef stew pieces, cut into strips

1 small onion, minced

2 cloves garlic, pressed

½ cup mushroom caps, sliced

1½ cups beef broth

¼ cup dry sherry

1 tablespoon Worcestershire sauce

¼ cup flour

½ cup sour cream

Salt and pepper to taste

1. Heat olive oil in the skillet over medium-high heat. Add the beef slices so they fit in the skillet (or work in batches). Fry them in the skillet turning so that all sides get browned, about 3 minutes. Transfer the beef pieces to a plate and cover with foil to keep warm.
2. Add a bit more oil if necessary, and saute the onion, garlic, and mushrooms until soft, about 5 minutes. In the skillet, add the beef broth, sherry, and Worcestershire sauce. Bring to a boil, scraping the browned bits of meat and vegetables off the bottom of the pan. Put the flour in a bowl and add some of the heated sauce, using a whisk to form a paste. Add a bit more sauce to the bowl, and when the sauce is incorporated with the flour, stir all of it into the skillet and mix. Continue to cook until the sauce thickens somewhat.
3. Reduce the heat and add the sour cream. Add the meat pieces back to the skillet. When everything is hot, serve. Season with salt and pepper.

This dish must be served over egg noodles. Nothing else will do. Chop some fresh parsley to use as a garnish if desired, and have some bread available to lap up the extra sauce.

SAUSAGE AND PEPPERS

SERVES 4 TO 6 ✦ ACTIVE TIME: 40 MINUTES ✦ START TO FINISH: 60 MINUTES

This combination is so delicious. It includes onions, as well. Saute everything until it is crispy and caramelized, and serve the sausages in large sandwich rolls.

4 tablespoons olive oil

1 pound sweet Italian sausages

4 cloves garlic, sliced thin

2 green bell peppers, ribs and seeds removed, sliced thin

1 red bell pepper, ribs and seeds removed, sliced thin

2 hot peppers like Italian, Poblano, or Hungarian hot wax (or 1 jalapeno), ribs and seeds removed, sliced thin

1 large onion, sliced thin

Salt and pepper to taste

1. Preheat oven to 350 degrees.
2. Heat the skillet over medium-high heat. Add 1 tablespoon of olive oil. Saute the sausages in the oil until golden brown on all sides—about 3 minutes a side. Transfer the sausages to a plate.
3. Add the additional oil, and add the garlic, peppers, and onion. Cook, stirring, while vegetables soften, about 5 to 6 minutes. Return the sausages to the skillet.
4. Put the skillet in the oven and bake for about 15 minutes, until sausages are cooked through and vegetables are tender and slightly crunchy on the outsides. Season with salt and pepper. Serve with long sandwich buns, and hot pepper flakes if desired.

SIMPLE SKILLET SALMON

SERVES 4 TO 6 **ACTIVE TIME: 20 MINUTES** **START TO FINISH: 30 MINUTES**

Start with super-fresh fish, and keep it simple—butter, lemon, salt, and pepper—and you can create a succulent dish that is ready in no time.

3 to 4 pounds salmon filets

2 tablespoons unsalted butter, cut in pieces, softened

1 lemon

Salt and pepper

1 tablespoon oil

Rinse the filets with cold water to ensure that any scales or bones are removed. Dry them in paper towels. Rub soft butter on both sides of the filets, squeeze lemon over them, and season with salt and pepper.

Heat the skillet over medium-high heat and add the tablespoon of olive oil. Add the filets, flesh side down. Cook on one side for about 3 minutes, then flip them and cook only 2 minutes on the other side. Remove the pan from the heat and let the fish rest in it for a minute before serving. The skin should peel right off.

There are different cuts of salmon: steaks and filets. The steaks are cut from the meat around the backbone, and they contain that bone in the middle. Filets are cut from the flesh that extends from the head to the tail of the fish. For this recipe, use filets.

BLACKENED TILAPIA

SERVES 4 ✦ ACTIVE TIME: 40 MINUTES ✦ START TO FINISH: 90 MINUTES

The cast-iron skillet is perfect for blackening fish, as blackening requires high heat and quick cooking. Although the result is delicious, the blackening process creates a lot of smoke, so be sure to turn the oven fan on or open the windows.

1 stick melted butter

4 boneless tilapia fillets, about 4 oz. each

1 lemon, cut into 4 wedges

Blackened Seasoning

2 tablespoons paprika

1 tablespoons onion powder

3 tablespoons garlic powder

2 tablespoons cayenne pepper

1 tablespoons white pepper

1½ tablespoons finely ground black pepper

1 tablespoon dried thyme

1 tablespoon dried oregano

1 tablespoon ground chipotle chile

1. In a bowl, combine all the spices for your blackened seasoning and set aside.
2. Heat the skillet over high heat for about 10 minutes until very hot. While the skillet heats, rinse the fillets and then pat dry with paper towels. Dip the fish fillets in the melted butter, covering both sides, and then press the blackened seasoning generously into both sides.
3. Put the fish in the skillet and cook for about 3 minutes a side, placing a bit of butter on the tops while the bottoms cook. Serve with lemon.

Tilapia is a wonderful fish for blackening, as it is a firm-fleshed fish that is fairly bland and thus benefits from seasoning. You can blacken any kind of fish, though. Others that taste great prepared this way are catfish, tuna, grouper, halibut, trout, and even shrimp.

ROASTED TROUT WITH FENNEL AND ONION

SERVES 2 **ACTIVE TIME: 60 MINUTES** **START TO FINISH: 2 HOURS**

Roasting the whole trout on a bed of onions and fennel creates a sweetness of flavor and crispness of skin that make for a flavorful and satisfying—and very nutritious—meal.

2 tablespoons olive oil

2 onions, sliced thin

2 heads of fennel, fronds removed, sliced thin

2 brook trout, about 1 pound total, cleaned

Salt and pepper

Lemon

Preheat the oven to 450 degrees.

Heat the skillet over medium-high heat. In a bowl, mix the onions and fennel in the olive oil. Add the vegetables to the skillet and cook, stirring, until they soften and start to brown, about 20 minutes. Flatten and spread the vegetables in the skillet. Lightly oil the fish on both sides, season with salt and pepper, and place the fish on the bed of vegetables.

Put the skillet in the oven and bake for 25 minutes.

To serve, remove the fish from the skillet and filet them by making an incision from head to tail, holding the head firmly, and lifting gently to pull the skeleton away from the bottom of the fish. Once boned, put the filets on a plate and serve with the vegetables on the side. Garnish with lemon.

BLACK BEAN BURGERS

SERVES 4 ✦ ACTIVE TIME: 90 MINUTES ✦ START TO FINISH: 2 HOURS

For those times when you want to take a break from meat but want the great taste and texture of a juicy hamburger, try making these black bean burgers. Be sure you have ripe tomatoes and avocadoes to put on them when serving.

1 (15-oz.) can black beans, drained and rinsed

⅓ cup scallions

¼ cup chopped roasted red peppers

¼ cup cooked corn

¼ cup breadcrumbs (plain)

1 egg, lightly beaten

2 tablespoons cilantro, chopped

½ teaspoon cumin

½ teaspoon cayenne pepper

½ teaspoon freshly ground black pepper

1 teaspoon fresh-squeezed lime juice

1 tablespoon olive oil

Hamburger buns

Tomato slices

Avocado slices

Red onion, thin slices

1. In a food processor or blender, combine half the beans with the scallions and roasted red peppers. Pulse to blend until you have a thick paste. Transfer to a large bowl.
2. Add the corn, breadcrumbs, egg, cilantro, cumin, cayenne, pepper, and lime juice. Stir to blend. Add the remaining beans and stir vigorously to get all ingredients to stick together. Cover bowl with plastic wrap and let sit at room temperature for about ½ hour.
3. Heat skillet over medium-high heat. Form mixture into 4 to 6 patties. Add oil to skillet and, when hot, add the patties. Cook, covered, about 5 minutes per side.
4. Serve immediately on hamburger buns with slices of tomato, avocado, and red onion.

VEAL PARMIGIANA

MAKES 4 VEAL CUTLETS ✦ ACTIVE TIME: 30 MINUTES ✦ START TO FINISH: 60 MINUTES

What I like about using veal cutlets for this dish is that they are thinner (and leaner) than chicken cutlets, with a bigger flavor, too. Use fresh mozzarella and shred it yourself; it tastes much better. And of course, don't forget hot pepper flakes on the side!

½ cup flour

Salt and pepper

½ cup breadcrumbs (Italian seasoned)

¼ cup grated Parmesan cheese

1 egg

½ cup milk

4 veal cutlets

3 tablespoons olive oil

2 cloves garlic, peeled and cut in half

4 oz. mozzarella, shredded

1 (24-oz.) jar marinara sauce (or 3 cups homemade)

1. Preheat the oven to 450 degrees.
2. In a shallow bowl, season the flour with salt and pepper.
3. In another shallow bowl, mix the breadcrumbs and Parmesan cheese.
4. In a third shallow bowl, whisk the egg with the milk until combined.
5. Line a plate with wax paper. Dip the cutlets in flour, then egg/milk, then breadcrumb mix, coating both sides. Place the breaded cutlets on the wax paper until ready to cook.
6. Heat the skillet over medium-high heat and add the olive oil. When it's hot, add the olive oil and the garlic pieces. Brown the cutlets in the oil, cooking for 2 to 3 minutes per side. Remove the wax paper, and put the cutlets on the plate.
7. Lower the heat to medium and add the marinara sauce, stirring until sauce bubbles. Reduce heat to low and simmer for about 10 minutes.
8. Put the cutlets in the skillet and sprinkle with additional Parmesan. Divide the shredded mozzarella between the cutlets, put it on top of each, and put the skillet in the oven. Cook until cheese melts and begins to brown, about 5 minutes. Serve immediately.

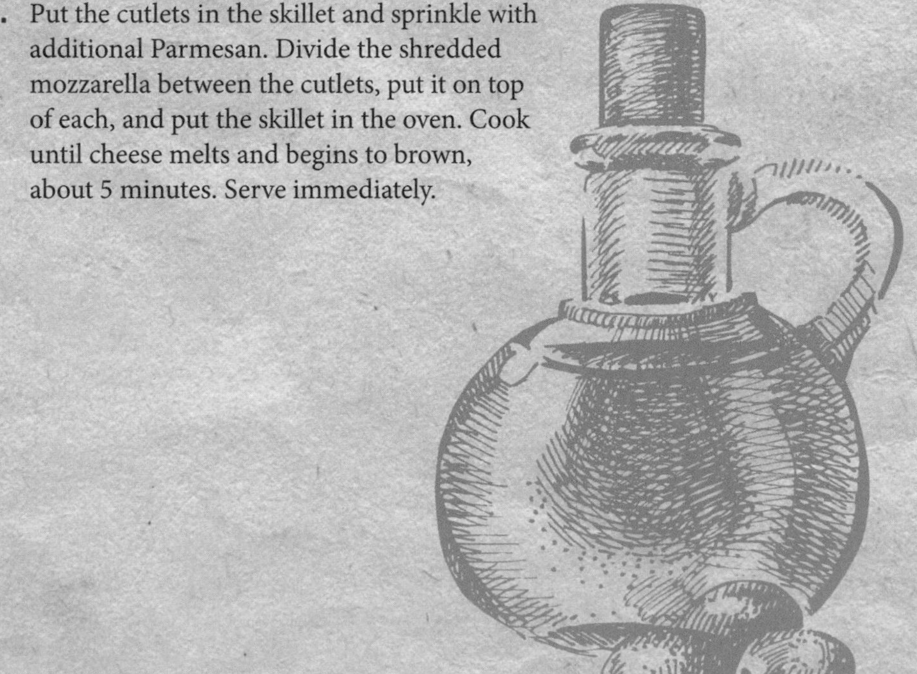

VEAL FRANCESE

MAKES 4 CUTLETS ✦ ACTIVE TIME: 30 MINUTES ✦ START TO FINISH: 45 MINUTES

If veal Parmigiana is a down-to-earth comfort food, rich with tomatoes and cheese, then veal Francese is the elegant uptowner, with a nuanced sauce of butter, lemon, and wine. If given a choice, I'd take both.

1 pound veal cutlets

Salt and pepper

¼ cup flour

1 egg

1 lemon, cut in half, seeds removed

2 tablespoons butter

1 tablespoon vegetable oil

2 cloves garlic, peeled and sliced in half

⅓ cup dry white wine

1. In a shallow bowl, season the flour with salt and pepper. Put the egg in a separate shallow bowl and beat in 1 tablespoon of fresh-squeezed lemon juice.
2. Heat the skillet over medium-high heat. Add the butter and oil together. When melted, add the garlic slices and stir. Dip a cutlet in the egg blend, then in the flour, coating lightly on both sides. Put the cutlet in the skillet. Do the same with the remaining cutlets. Saute for just a couple of minutes each side, until lightly browned, and transfer to a plate.
3. With the heat lowered to medium, squeeze the juice from half the lemon into the skillet, then add the wine. Increase the heat and bring the liquid to a rolling boil, stirring the browned bits up from the bottom. Cook the sauce so that it reduces and lightens as it boils, about 5 minutes.
4. To serve, dip the cutlets in the sauce, put on a plate, and pass the extra sauce at the table.

SKILLET WINGS

MAKES 3 TO 6 SERVINGS ✦ ACTIVE TIME: 30 MINUTES ✦ START TO FINISH: 60 MINUTES

These are a double whammy of sauteed goodness baked to perfection in a very hot oven. Invite over your wing-loving friends and see if they don't agree that these are the best ever.

6 whole chicken wings

1 tablespoon butter

1 tablespoon vegetable oil

Salt and pepper for seasoning

⅛ teaspoon cayenne pepper

7 oz. Frank's Red Hot sauce

1. Preheat the oven to 500 degrees.
2. With a sharp knife, cut the wings at the joint so that you have three sections: the single-boned section, the double-boned section, and the tip. Discard the tips.
3. When the oven is almost to 500 degrees, put the skillet over medium-high heat and add the butter and oil. When this gets hot, add the wing sections and stir. Season with salt and pepper, sprinkle with cayenne, stir again, then coat the wings with a portion of the hot sauce (use just enough to coat the wings).
4. Put the skillet in the oven. Cook the wings for a couple of minutes, remove the skillet (wear oven mitts!), flip over each wing section, and coat with additional hot sauce. Put the skillet back in the oven and cook for another 2 minutes. Repeat this procedure for about 20 minutes, basting with the hot sauce in the skillet, until the wings are fully cooked and crispy all over.
5. Serve with the traditional blue cheese dip and a side of celery and carrot sticks.

If you like fiery wings, you'll want to up the heat in this recipe. Instead of Frank's Red Hot sauce and a hint of cayenne pepper, look for the kicked-up styles of Frank's, including a hot wing sauce and an extra-hot sauce. If you have a favorite hot sauce besides Frank's, give it a try. The secret to these great wings is the sautéing then baking.

GENERAL TSO CHICKEN

SERVES 4 **ACTIVE TIME: 1½ HOURS** **START TO FINISH: 2 HOURS**

When our family goes for Chinese food, someone always orders this dish. I got curious about how it could be made at home, since it seems a natural for the cooking ability of the cast-iron skillet. This recipe works—and it includes one of our favorite sauces, Sriracha!

1 large egg

1½ teaspoons toasted sesame oil

¼ cup + 1 tablespoon low-sodium soy sauce

¼ cup + 1 tablespoon cornstarch

1 pound skinless, boneless chicken thighs, cut into bite-sized pieces

1 tablespoon vegetable oil, plus more for frying

2 tablespoons fresh ginger, chopped fine

3 cloves garlic, minced

1 cup chicken broth

2 teaspoons Sriracha

3 tablespoons sugar

3 scallions, sliced thin

Carefully crack the egg over a medium-sized bowl, separating the white and yolk so the white goes into the bowl. Put the yolk in a cup and refrigerate for another use. Add the sesame oil, 1 tablespoon of soy sauce, and ¼ cup cornstarch. Whisk to combine. Add the chicken pieces and marinate at room temperature for about 30 minutes.

In a small skillet or saucepan, heat the tablespoon of oil over medium-high heat. Add the ginger and garlic and stir for about a minute. Add in the broth, Sriracha, sugar, remaining soy sauce, and tablespoon of cornstarch, whisking to combine the ingredients. Continue to whisk will cooking the sauce until it gets thick and glossy. Reduce the heat to low and cover to keep it warm.

Heat the cast iron skillet over medium-high heat and add about ½ inch of oil. When hot, add the chicken one piece at a time so it doesn't splatter too much. Turn the pieces with a slotted spoon so that they brown on all sides. Cook until crispy, about 5 minutes. As the pieces are cooked, transfer them to a plate lined with paper towels to drain.

When all the pieces are cooked, stir them with the scallions into the sauce. Serve hot.

This dish is usually served with a bowl of white rice and a side of steamed broccoli. We prefer brown rice, but we do think steamed broccoli makes the meal. To coordinate the three parts, make the rice ahead of time and reheat on the stove over a low flame. The broccoli can be partially steamed ahead of time and then finished with additional steaming of about 10 minutes.

CHICKEN QUESADILLAS

SERVES 4 ✦ ACTIVE TIME: 45 MINUTES ✦ START TO FINISH: 90 MINUTES

This is a recipe that can be taken in many different directions with delicious results every time. It's all about what you have left over in your refrigerator, and a little skillet magic. *To make your own tortillas, see page 191.*

3 tablespoons olive oil

1 red onion, sliced thin

1 clove garlic, minced

3 cups cooked chicken, diced

4 (8-inch) corn or flour tortillas

2 cups shredded sharp cheddar cheese

½ cup pitted black olives, sliced thin

½ cup salsa

1 avocado, peeled, pit removed, and sliced thin

1. Heat a 12-inch skillet over medium-high heat and add 2 tablespoons of olive oil, tilting to coat the pan as it heats. Add the onion and garlic and cook, stirring, until onion is translucent, about 3 minutes. Add cooked chicken and stir to combine and warm the chicken. Transfer to a bowl, cover with foil, and keep warm.
2. Wipe skillet clean with a paper towel, return to heat, and add a tablespoon of oil, coating the pan. Add two tortillas, folded in half. Fill each half with the chicken mixture, and add some cheese, olives, salsa, and avocado. Fold the top down on each tortilla and press, cooking the bottom. Flip the tortillas and continue to cook for about 5 minutes.
3. Keep cooked quesadillas warm in the oven while you cook through the batch. Serve warm with additional salsa on the side.

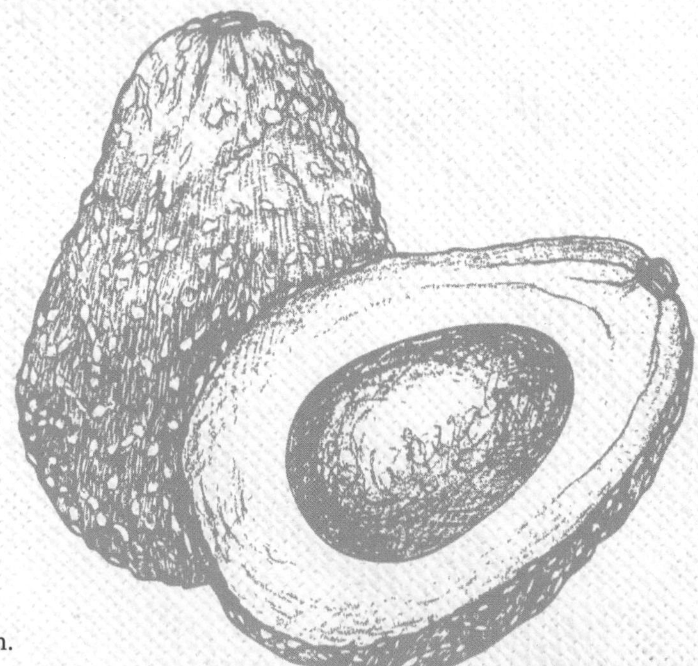

Variations

- Substitute sliced leftover steak for the chicken.
- Substitute sliced jalapenos for the olives, or include both.
- Drizzle with Sriracha before serving.
- Serve with lime slices to squeeze over the quesadillas, especially if spicy.

SIDE DISHES

Truthfully, this chapter could be a book in itself. In my opinion, this is where a lot of the magic happens in cooking—especially with a cast-iron skillet—because there are so many ingredients to play with. Vegetables, starches, grains, spices, sauces—you'll see what I mean when you thumb through this chapter. Deliciousness happens over and over, and with simple ingredients that are easy to find, affordable, and satisfying for the whole family.

STUFFED TOMATOES

MAKES 6 SERVINGS ✦ ACTIVE TIME: 1 HOUR ✦ START TO FINISH: 2 HOURS

These are great filled with a stuffing with meat in it or without. The sidebar adapts the recipe for a meatless version.

6 ripe large tomatoes

1 pound sausage, casings removed

1 onion, diced

4 cloves garlic, minced

2 teaspoons red pepper flakes (optional)

8 white mushrooms, stems removed, diced

½ green bell pepper, seeds removed, diced

2 cups plain breadcrumbs

2 tablespoons dried sage

1 cup grated Parmesan cheese

Salt and pepper to taste

1. Preheat the oven to 375 degrees.
2. Core the tomatoes, and using a small paring knife or a serrated grapefruit spoon, scoop out the insides. Once hollowed, sprinkle salt on the insides and turn upside down on a plate covered with a paper towel to absorb the water. Let sit for about 30 minutes
3. Heat the skillet over medium-high heat and cook the sausage, breaking it up as it cooks. Cook until there is no pink showing in the meat. When cooked, transfer the sausage to a large bowl using a slotted spoon. In the sausage fat, cook the onion and garlic until translucent, about 4 minutes. Add the mushrooms and peppers and continue to cook, over medium heat, stirring, until vegetables soften, about 10 minutes. Add red pepper flakes if desired.
4. Add the mushroom mixture to the sausage and combine. Then add the breadcrumbs, sage, and Parmesan. Season to taste with salt and pepper.
5. Wipe down the skillet and brush with olive oil. Position the tomatoes in the skillet bottoms down. Start filling the tomatoes gently, dividing the filling between them. Cover the tomatoes with aluminum foil and put the skillet in the oven. Bake for about 30 minutes, remove the foil, and continue baking for another 10 to 15 minutes until cooked through. Serve hot.

Meatless Stuffed Tomatoes: If you want to make this without sausage, simply omit that ingredient. Double the amount of mushrooms, and after sautéeing the mushrooms and peppers, drain the excess liquid. You can also add toasted walnut pieces for additional flavor and fiber.

RATATOUILLE

SERVES 4 ✦ ACTIVE TIME: 40 MINUTES ✦ START TO FINISH: 2 HOURS

There are variations on this dish—some insist that zucchini is a necessary ingredient—but I like it with just eggplant, peppers, and tomatoes—and garlic, of course.

⅓ cup olive oil

6 cloves garlic, minced

1 medium eggplant, cut into bite-sized cubes

2 peppers, seeded and diced

4 tomatoes, seeded and chopped

Salt and pepper to taste

1. Heat half the olive oil in the skillet over medium-high heat. Add the garlic and eggplant and cook, stirring, until pieces are coated with oil and just starting to cook, about 2 minutes. Reduce the heat slightly and add the peppers and additional oil, stirring to combine. With the heat on medium, cover the skillet and let cook, stirring every few minutes to be sure vegetables aren't sticking to the bottom of the pan. If the mix seems to dry, add a little more olive oil. As the eggplant softens, the dish will regain moisture.
2. After about 15 minutes, when the eggplant and peppers are nearly soft, add the tomatoes and stir to combine. With the lid off, continue to cook the ratatouille, stirring occasionally, until the eggplant and peppers are soft and the tomatoes are wilted. Remove the skillet from the heat, season with salt and pepper, and allow to sit for at least 1 hour. Reheat and eat.

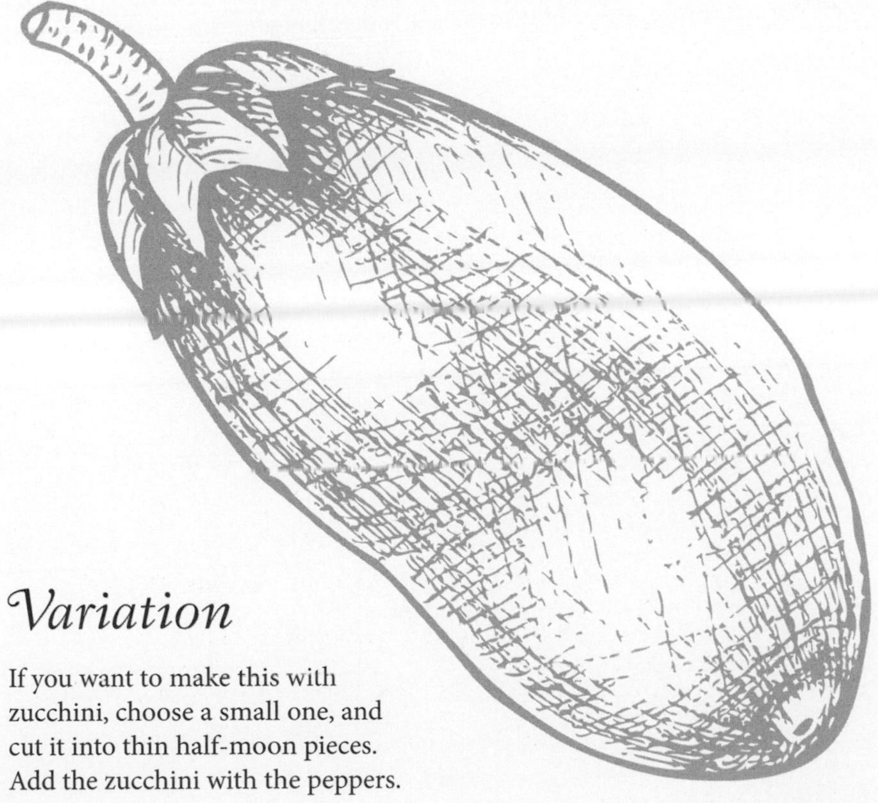

Variation

If you want to make this with zucchini, choose a small one, and cut it into thin half-moon pieces. Add the zucchini with the peppers.

SWEET POTATO PANCAKES

MAKES 6 TO 8 SERVINGS ✦ ACTIVE TIME: 60 MINUTES ✦ START TO FINISH: 90 MINUTES

Sweet potatoes aren't as moist as russet potatoes, so you won't need as much draining time with them. You will need to chop them finer to make more of a dough with them. Experiment until you get the right consistency.

6 large sweet potatoes, washed and peeled

1 large onion

3 eggs, beaten

½ cup matzoh meal

½ teaspoon sugar

Salt and freshly ground pepper

1 cup canola or vegetable oil

1. Using a hand grater or a food processor with a shredding attachment, grate the potatoes onto a large baking dish, and then transfer to a colander in the sink.
2. Grate the onion or use a knife to process into a very fine dice. Put the grated onion into a bowl.
3. Squeeze as much liquid out of the potatoes as possible.
4. Combine the potatoes and onion and begin processing in a food processor or blender to turn the vegetables into a rough puree. Don't overblend or chop, as the mix will get too starchy.
5. Squeeze the puree through a fine-sieved colander to get out excess liquid, then let the mix sit and drain on its own for about 20 to 30 minutes.
6. Put the puree into a large bowl, and add the eggs, matzoh meal and sugar. Stir to thoroughly combine. Season with salt and pepper.
7. Heat the skillet over medium-high heat and add the oil. Be careful making the pancakes, as the oil can splatter. Take spoonfuls of the potato mix and place them in the oil. Cook for about 3 minutes a side. The pancakes should be golden brown on the outside and cooked through on the inside. You may need to adjust the temperature of the oil to get the right cooking temperature, especially if you have more than three in the skillet at one time.
8. When cooked, transfer with a slotted spoon to a plate lined with paper towels. Keep warm until ready to eat. Season with additional salt and pepper.

These pancakes will probably not hold together as well as regular potato pancakes, but they are equally yummy and versatile. Serve with pesto, or refried beans, or put some on a baking sheet, top with grated mozzarella, and broil for a couple of minutes to melt the cheese.

CRAZY-GOOD CABBAGE

MAKES 4 TO 6 SERVINGS ✦ ACTIVE TIME: 30 MINUTES ✦ START TO FINISH: 60 MINUTES

This Southern-inspired dish is a colorful blend of pale green cabbage, bright green peppers, deep red tomatoes, and bright yellow corn—with a cayenne kick!

2 tablespoons olive oil

1 medium head cabbage, cored and shredded

1 green pepper, seeds and ribs removed, diced

1 medium onion, diced

3 cups fresh tomatoes, seeds removed, chopped

1 ear corn, kernels removed, or 1 (8-oz.) can kernels, drained

1 teaspoon cayenne pepper

Salt and pepper to taste

1. Heat the skillet over medium-high heat and add the oil. Add cabbage, peppers, and onions and stir, cooking, until onions become translucent, about 3 minutes. Add the tomatoes, corn, and cayenne and stir. Season with salt and pepper.
2. Cover, reduce the heat to low, and simmer until the cabbage is cooked through, about 30 minutes. Stir occasionally. Serve hot with extra salt, pepper, and cayenne.

CARAWAY SEED CABBAGE

MAKES 4 TO 6 SERVINGS ✦ ACTIVE TIME: 30 MINUTES ✦ START TO FINISH: 60 MINUTES

If you prefer a more Eastern European flavor to your cabbage, try this variation.

2 tablespoons olive oil

1 medium head cabbage, cored and shredded

½ medium onion, diced

1 teaspoon toasted caraway seeds

Salt and pepper to taste

1. Heat the skillet over medium-high heat and add the oil. Add cabbage, onions and toasted caraway seeds, cooking until onions become translucent, about 3 minutes. Season with salt and pepper.
2. Cover, reduce the heat to low, and simmer until the cabbage is cooked through, about 30 minutes. Stir occasionally. Serve hot with extra salt and pepper.

SPINACH AND SHALLOTS

SERVES 6 TO 8 ✦ ACTIVE TIME: 25 MINUTES ✦ START TO FINISH: 40 MINUTES

Using mellow-flavored shallots instead of the usual garlic and onions keeps the spinach flavor bright in this quick-cooking dish. A splash of balsamic vinegar takes it over the top.

3 tablespoons olive oil

4 large shallots, sliced thin

2 pounds fresh spinach, tough stems removed, rinsed, and thoroughly dried

1 tablespoon balsamic vinegar

Salt and pepper

1. Heat skillet over medium-high heat. Add olive oil and shallots and cook, stirring, until shallots are translucent, about 2 minutes.
2. Add the spinach and cook, stirring, until all the leaves are covered in the oil/onion mix, another 2 or 3 minutes. The spinach will start to reduce quickly. Reduce the heat and keep stirring so none of it burns. If desired, you can turn the heat to low and cover the skillet so the leaves steam-cook.
3. When the spinach leaves are wilted and still bright green, splash them with the balsamic vinegar, shaking the pan to distribute. Season with salt and pepper and serve.

This dish works best with more mature spinach. Reserve baby spinach greens for salads and use the larger leaves for this dish.

Variation

If you prefer less onion flavor, use two shallots instead of four.

CREAMED CORN

MAKES 8 TO 10 SERVINGS ✦ ACTIVE TIME: 30 MINUTES ✦ START TO FINISH: 60 MINUTES

Take advantage of the season when fresh corn is plentiful. This is a nice alternative to corn on the cob and uses a lot of corn.

12 ears fresh corn

3 tablespoons butter

1 cup water

1 cup half-and-half

½ teaspoon salt

Freshly ground black pepper

3 tablespoons flour

½ cup warm water

1. Shuck the corn and remove all strands of silk. Rinse the ears and shake to dry.
2. Standing each ear up in the middle of a large baking dish, use a sharp knife to cut down the sides and remove all the kernels. With the kernels off, take the blade of a dull knife and press it along each side of the ear to "milk" the cob of the liquid. Discard the milked cobs.
3. Heat the skillet over medium heat and, when hot, lower the heat and add the butter so it melts slowly. When melted, add the corn kernels and milk from the cobs and stir to coat them with the butter. Increase the heat to medium-high and add the water and half-and-half. Bring to a boil, stirring constantly, and when bubbling, reduce to low heat. Add the salt and pepper.
4. In a measuring cup, add the warm water to the flour and mix until thoroughly combined. Drizzle the flour mixture into the corn, stirring and continuing to cook on low until the sauce thickens. If it gets too thick, add some more water or whole milk. Serve hot.

You'll want to freeze some of this to enjoy in the dead of winter. It's easy. Allow the creamed corn to cool, put it in airtight containers, being sure to push all the air out, seal the container, and it's ready to go to the freezer. Put the date it was cooked on the container so you remember.

SAUTÉED CHERRY TOMATOES

SERVES 4 ✦ ACTIVE TIME: 25 MINUTES ✦ START TO FINISH: 25 MINUTES

Fresh rosemary adds lovely fragrance and flavor to this dish, which is a great way to cook up a pint of grape tomatoes or cherry tomatoes from the farmer's market or the grocery store. So easy!

1 pint cherry (grape) tomatoes

1 tablespoon olive oil

1 clove garlic, minced

½ teaspoon salt

Freshly ground black pepper

2 teaspoons fresh rosemary

1. Preheat the oven to 450 degrees.
2. In a bowl, toss the cherry tomatoes in with the oil, garlic, salt and pepper. Transfer to the skillet.
3. Roast in the oven for 10 minutes, remove the skillet and shake the tomatoes around. Return to the oven and roast for another 5 minutes. Remove and shake, sprinkle with the rosemary, then return to the oven for another 5 minutes until the tomatoes are charred.
4. Serve hot and season with additional salt and pepper if desired.

I like to serve these roasted tomatoes with rosemary alongside grilled chicken with lemon and garlic and wild rice—followed by a lemon dessert like Lemon Cake (page 237).

ROASTED CAULIFLOWER STEAKS

MAKES 4 TO 6 SERVINGS **ACTIVE TIME: 30 MINUTES** **START TO FINISH: 60 MINUTES**

There's something about roasting cauliflower that accentuates its somewhat sweet, nutty flavor. Season it with warm, earthy spices like cumin and turmeric, and you have a delicious alternative to a starchy side, full of flavor and nutrition.

1½ tablespoons olive oil

1 teaspoon salt

Freshly ground pepper

½ teaspoon ground cumin

½ teaspoon ground coriander

½ teaspoon turmeric

¼ teaspoon cayenne pepper

1 medium head of cauliflower, stem and green leaves removed

Preheat the oven to 425 degrees.

In a bowl, combine the oil, salt, pepper, and spices and whisk to mix thoroughly.

Cut the cauliflower cross-wise into ½-inch slices. Put the slices in the skillet and brush the tops liberally with oil mixture. Turn the "steaks" over and brush the other side.

Put the skillet in the oven and roast for about 20 minutes, turning the pieces over after 10 minutes. A toothpick inserted in the flesh should go in easily to indicate that the cauliflower is cooked through.

Serve the slices hot, with a side of crème fraiche or sour cream if desired.

This recipe can be made with cauliflower florets, too. Instead of slicing the cauliflower into cross sections, just pick off the florets. Put them in the bowl of seasoned oil and toss to coat. Put the florets in the skillet and bake, shaking the pan halfway through to turn the pieces.

POTATO PANCAKES

MAKES 6 TO 8 SERVINGS ✦ ACTIVE TIME: 60 MINUTES ✦ START TO FINISH: 90 MINUTES

The way to make the best-tasting potato pancakes is to get as much liquid out of the grated potatoes and onions as possible. This is a bit time-consuming, but it's worth it! You can also prepare the potato-onion mixture a day or two earlier and keep the mix in an airtight container in the refrigerator.

6 large russet potatoes, washed and peeled

1 large onion

3 eggs, beaten

¼ to ½ cup matzoh meal

Salt and freshly ground pepper

1 cup canola or vegetable oil

1. Using a hand grater or a food processor with a shredding attachment, grate the potatoes onto a large baking dish, and then transfer to a colander in the sink.
2. Grate the onion or use a knife to process into a very fine dice. Put the grated onion into a bowl.
3. Squeeze as much liquid out of the potatoes as possible. Take half of the grated potatoes, mix them with the onions, and process the mixture in a food processor or blender to create a rough puree. Don't overblend or chop, as the mix will get too starchy.
4. Put the puree in a separate colander so that it can drain. Let both colanders drain for another 20 to 30 minutes. Push down on both to release more liquid and squeeze them again before continuing with the recipe.
5. Combine the two batches into a large bowl, and add the eggs and matzoh meal. Stir to thoroughly combine. Season with salt and pepper.
6. Heat the skillet over medium-high heat and add the oil. Be careful making the pancakes, as the oil can splatter. Take spoonfuls of the potato mix and place them in the oil. Cook for about 3 minutes a side. The pancakes should be golden brown on the outside and cooked through on the inside. You may need to adjust the temperature of the oil to get the right cooking temperature, especially if you have more than three in the skillet at one time.
7. When cooked, transfer with a slotted spoon to a plate lined with paper towels. Keep warm until ready to eat. Season with additional salt and pepper.

Variations

- Serve with chunky unsweetened applesauce and a small dollop of sour cream.
- Serve as you would French fries—with salt and vinegar, with ketchup, with gravy, or with salsa.
- For a nontraditional taco, top potato pancakes with chili and cheese.

CRISP-TENDER ASPARAGUS

SERVES 4 ✦ ACTIVE TIME: 20 MINUTES ✦ START TO FINISH: 30 MINUTES

Making asparagus in the skillet is almost like making them on the grill. The outsides are crisp while the insides are tender—perfect!

1 bunch thin asparagus

3 tablespoons olive oil

1 clove garlic, minced

½ teaspoon salt

½ teaspoon freshly ground pepper

Lemon wedges on the side

1. Cut the tough ends off the asparagus and rinse the rest.
2. Heat the skillet over medium-high heat. When hot, add the oil and let that get hot. Add the asparagus. Using tongs, keep picking up and turning them so they are cooked evenly in the oil. Cook the asparagus until they are bright green, hot on the outside but tender on the inside.
3. Add the garlic and the salt and pepper, and shake the pan around to distribute evenly. Cook for another 2 minutes. Transfer to a serving platter and serve with the lemon wedges.

The thinner the asparagus, the faster they'll cook. If you are working with super-fresh, thin stalks, you may need to reduce the cooking times in the recipe. On the other hand, if you're using vegetables that are thicker and maybe not as fresh, the cooking times should be fine, or may even need to increase.

FRIED OKRA

MAKES 4 TO 6 SERVINGS ✦ ACTIVE TIME: 30 MINUTES ✦ START TO FINISH: 60 MINUTES

Breaded in cornmeal and fried in the skillet, these okra are hot and moist on the inside, crunchy on the outside—better than French fries.

1 egg, beaten

½ cup milk

1 cup cornmeal

1 tablespoon flour

¾ teaspoons salt

½ teaspoon freshly ground black pepper

1 pound fresh okra, sliced into ½-inch-thick rounds

2 cups canola oil

Red pepper flakes to taste (optional)

Sea salt to taste (optional)

1. Preheat the oven to 225 degrees.
2. In a large bowl, whisk together the egg and milk until they are thoroughly combined. In another bowl, whisk together the cornmeal, flour, salt, and pepper. Add the okra to the egg mixture and toss until it is coated. Add half the cornmeal/flour mixture and toss, coating the pieces. Then add the remaining flour mix and toss again. This helps distribute the coating evenly.
3. Heat the oil in a skillet over medium-high heat.
4. Gently scoop a quantity of the breaded okra into the hot oil and fry them, turning with a slotted spoon and being careful not to dislodge the breading. Shake the pan if necessary, but watch the hot oil. Cook until golden all over, about 3 minutes per batch. Transfer the fried pieces to a platter covered with paper towels and keep them warm in the oven. Continue frying in batches until all are cooked.
5. Put the okra in a ceramic dish or bowl, and sprinkle with sea salt and red pepper flakes if desired.

BASIC BROCCOLI

MAKES 4 TO 6 SERVINGS ✦ ACTIVE TIME: 20 MINUTES ✦ START TO FINISH: 40 MINUTES

Roasting the broccoli brings out flavors you don't get when you boil or steam this vegetable. Play with the seasonings if you want, but first try it with just salt and pepper.

1 head of broccoli

2 tablespoons olive oil

Salt and freshly ground pepper

1. Preheat oven to 450 degrees.
2. Break florets off the broccoli to make bite-sized pieces. Cut the stems into ½-inch slices. Peel the tough layer off of the main stem, trim the top and bottom, and cut this into slices as well.
3. Wash and dry the pieces. Put them in a large bowl. Drizzle with the olive oil, and then stir the broccoli pieces in the oil to coat them. Season with salt and pepper.
4. Put the florets and stem pieces in the skillet and put in the oven. Bake for 25 to 30 minutes, stirring the pieces halfway through. Serve hot.

Variations

- Add a teaspoon of red pepper flakes.
- Use 1 tablespoon sesame oil and 1 tablespoon olive oil, and sprinkle with sesame seeds when cooked.
- Sprinkle with tamari after cooking (reduce salt due to sodium content of tamari).
- Add small pieces of blue cheese to the skillet when the broccoli is taken out of the oven the last time.

Using a cast-iron skillet has a surprising health benefit: The skillet actually leaches iron into your food, helping enhance your iron intake.

CORN FRITTERS

SERVES 4 ✦ ACTIVE TIME: 20 MINUTES ✦ START TO FINISH: 40 MINUTES

Sweet yet substantive, fancy yet simple, corn fritters are a family chef's best friend because they work no matter what the occasion.

1 egg, well beaten

1 teaspoon sugar

½ teaspoon salt

1 tablespoon butter, melted

2 teaspoons baking powder

1 cup flour

⅔ cup milk

2 cups cooked corn, cooled

1 tablespoon canola oil

1. In a large bowl, combine egg, sugar, salt, butter, baking powder, flour, and milk and stir thoroughly. Add the corn and mix.
2. Heat the skillet over medium-high heat and add the oil. Drop spoonfuls of batter into the skillet. Brown on both sides, about 3 minutes per side. Scoop out with a slotted spoon and put on a plate lined with paper towels to drain. Keep fritters warm while making more. Serve warm.

The best corn to use for this is leftover cooked corn on the cob that's been in the refrigerator overnight. Otherwise, you can take frozen corn and thaw the kernels, drying them before putting them in the batter. If you use canned corn, be sure all water is drained from it, and choose a high-quality brand so the kernels are firm and sweet, not mushy.

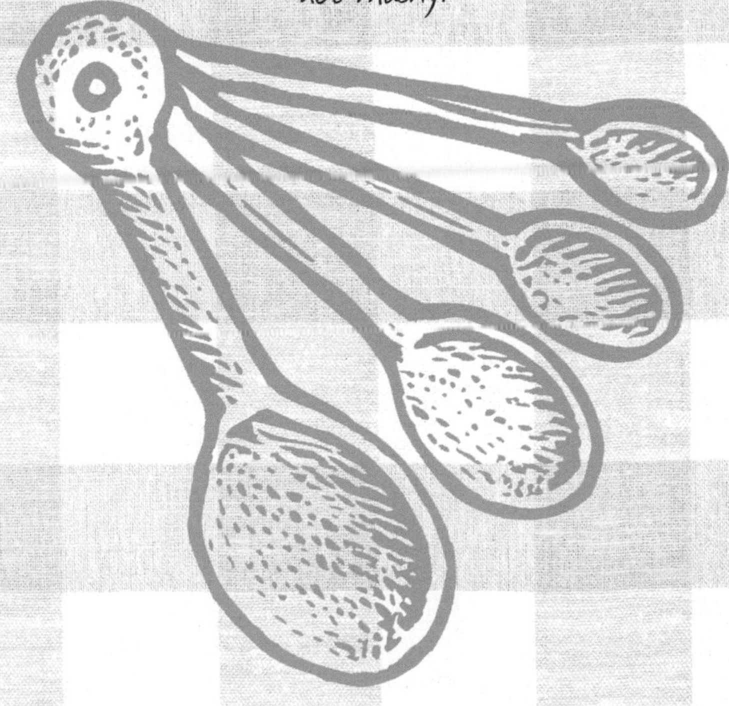

CORN FRITTERS WITH CORIANDER

MAKES 6 TO 8 SERVINGS ✦ ACTIVE TIME: 30 MINUTES ✦ START TO FINISH: 60 MINUTES

If you have the time and patience to make these the size of silver dollars, they are great for parties. Make a big stack of them and serve them warm with a variety of dipping sauces.

1 tablespoon olive oil

2 small shallots, minced

½ onion, diced

1 teaspoon fresh chopped ginger root

1 cup flour

1½ cups corn kernels

1 teaspoon ground cumin

½ cup water

2 eggs

½ cup coriander leaves, chopped fine (coarse stems removed)

½ teaspoon red pepper flakes

Salt and freshly ground pepper

⅓ cup olive oil (or less)

1. Preheat oven to 350 degrees.
2. Heat the skillet over medium-high heat. Add the oil, shallots, onion, and ginger and cook, stirring, until onion is translucent, about 2 minutes.
3. In a blender or food processor, place the flour, 1 cup of the corn, onion-ginger mix, cumin, water, and eggs. Process on low until well combined. Transfer to a large bowl and add the remaining corn, plus the shallots, coriander, and red pepper flakes. Season with salt and pepper.
4. Place the skillet back over the burner on medium-high heat. Add enough oil to coat the bottom. Make small fritters, cooking until browned on both sides, about 3 minutes a side. Transfer to a plate covered with paper towels to absorb extra oil. Keep warm, covered in foil, until ready to serve.

Variations

Serve these coriander-spice corn fritters with a variety of dipping sauces. Here are some good ones.

- **Curry-yogurt:** Into 1 cup of plain Greek yogurt, stir 1 tablespoon curry and ½ teaspoon fresh lime juice.
- **Creamy salsa:** Put 1 cup of your favorite tomato-based salsa in a small food processor and pulse until smooth. Transfer to a bowl, and add ½ to 1 cup sour cream. Add some diced jalapeno pepper to give it extra kick.
- **Harissa-studded olive oil:** Harissa is a North African pepper sauce that's becoming easier to find. Mix a heaping teaspoon in with a small bowl of extra-virgin olive oil for a spicy/smoky dip.

ROASTED ROOT VEGETABLES

MAKES 4 TO 6 SERVINGS ✦ ACTIVE TIME: 20 MINUTES ✦ START TO FINISH: 60 MINUTES

If you find yourself home from the farmer's market on a fall morning with bunches of root vegetables that looked so good at the market but are now baffling you as a cook, this recipe will save you.

2 small parsnips, trimmed and scrubbed clean

1 turnip, trimmed and scrubbed clean

4 small beets, trimmed and scrubbed clean

4 medium carrots, trimmed, scrubbed clean

½ onion, cut into slices

1 small bulb fennel, trimmed and cut into slivers

¼ cup olive oil

Salt and pepper to taste

2 teaspoons dried rosemary, crumbled

1. Preheat the oven to 400 degrees.
2. Cut the cleaned vegetables in half or quarters to form bite-sized pieces.
3. In a large bowl, combine all cut vegetables and pour the olive oil over them. Season with salt and pepper and toss to coat.
4. Put the vegetables in the skillet and sprinkle the rosemary over everything.
5. Put the skillet in the oven and bake for about 40 minutes, turning the vegetables over after the first 20 minutes. Serve warm.

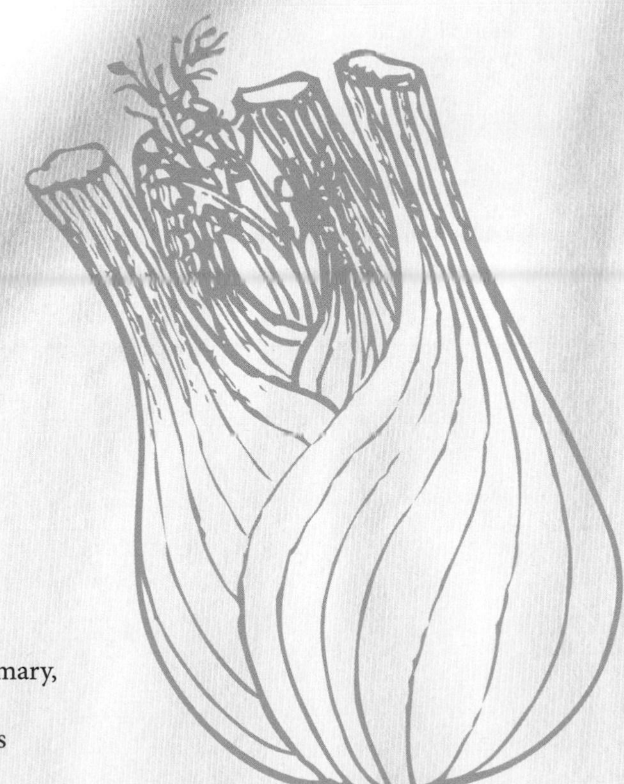

Variation

Substitute herbes de Provence for the rosemary. This is a French blend of rosemary, fennel, basil, thyme, marjoram, basil, tarragon, and lavender—all the goodness of a Provencal herb garden.

GLAZED CARROTS

SERVES 4 ✦ ACTIVE TIME: 20 MINUTES ✦ START TO FINISH: 40 MINUTES

Sugar brings out the best in already-sweet carrots, especially when it's part of a butter sauce.

1½ pounds carrots

¾ cup water

4 tablespoons butter

2 tablespoons sugar

Salt

Chopped fresh parsley

1. Peel and trim the carrots. Cut them in half and cut the halves in half length-wise.
2. Put the carrots in the skillet with the water, butter, and sugar. Bring to a boil over medium-high heat.
3. When boiling, reduce the heat to low and simmer for another 10 minutes, stirring the carrots occasionally.
4. When carrots are tender and there is a buttery sauce, sprinkle with salt. Garnish with the chopped parsley and serve.

Variation

Add some fiber to this dish by substituting sweet potatoes for half the carrots. Peel them and slice into spears the same size as those of the carrots. A dash of cayenne tastes good with this combination.

SKILLET EGGPLANT PARM

SERVES 4 ✦ ACTIVE TIME: 20 MINUTES ✦ START TO FINISH: 60 MINUTES

Gooey goodness straight from the skillet, rich with garlic, fresh mozzarella, and Parmesan cheese—and the eggplant isn't fried, so it's not too heavy.

1 large eggplant

Salt for sprinkling on eggplant

2 tablespoons olive oil

1 cup Italian seasoned breadcrumbs

2 tablespoons grated Parmesan cheese

1 egg, beaten

Prepared spaghetti sauce (no sugar or meat added)

2 cloves garlic, pressed through a garlic press

8 oz. mozzarella cheese, shredded

1. Preheat the oven to 350 degrees.
2. Trim the top and bottom off the eggplant and slice into ¼-inch slices. Put the slices on paper towels in a single layer, sprinkle salt over them, and leave them for about 15 minutes. Turn the slices over, salt this side, and let sit for another 15 minutes.
3. Rinse the salt from all the pieces and dry with clean paper towels.
4. Drizzle oil over a baking sheet in preparation for the eggplant.
5. In a shallow bowl, combine the breadcrumbs and Parmesan cheese. Put the beaten egg in another shallow bowl. Dip the slices of eggplant in egg, then breadcrumbs, coating both sides. Put them on the baking sheet.
6. Bake in the oven for about 10 minutes, turn them over, and bake another 10 minutes. Remove the sheet from the oven.
7. Put a layer of spaghetti sauce in the cast iron skillet and stir in the pressed garlic. Lay the eggplant slices in the sauce, layering to fit. Top with the shredded mozzarella.
8. Put the skillet in the oven and bake for about 30 minutes, until the sauce is bubbling and the cheese is golden. Allow to cool for about 10 minutes, then serve with extra sauce if desired.

ROASTED RED POTATOES WITH SEA SALT

SERVES 6 ✦ ACTIVE TIME: 20 MINUTES ✦ START TO FINISH: 60 MINUTES

The great thing about red potatoes is that the skins are very thin and don't need to be peeled off. They taste great, add extra fiber and vitamins, and look good, too.

12 to 14 small red potatoes, scrubbed clean

2 to 3 tablespoons olive oil

Freshly ground pepper

Coarse sea salt

Chopped fresh parsley

1. Preheat oven to 375 degrees.
2. In a bowl, drizzle the oil over the potatoes. Grind some fresh pepper on the potatoes. Put them in the skillet to form a single layer. Sprinkle the potatoes with sea salt.
3. Bake in the oven for 25 to 40 minutes, turning half way through the cooking time, until potatoes are cooked through. Serve hot with chopped parsley as a garnish.

Red potatoes are available in grocery stores most of the year. Baby potatoes harvested in late summer also taste fabulous prepared this way. Fingerling potatoes can be cut in half and roasted.

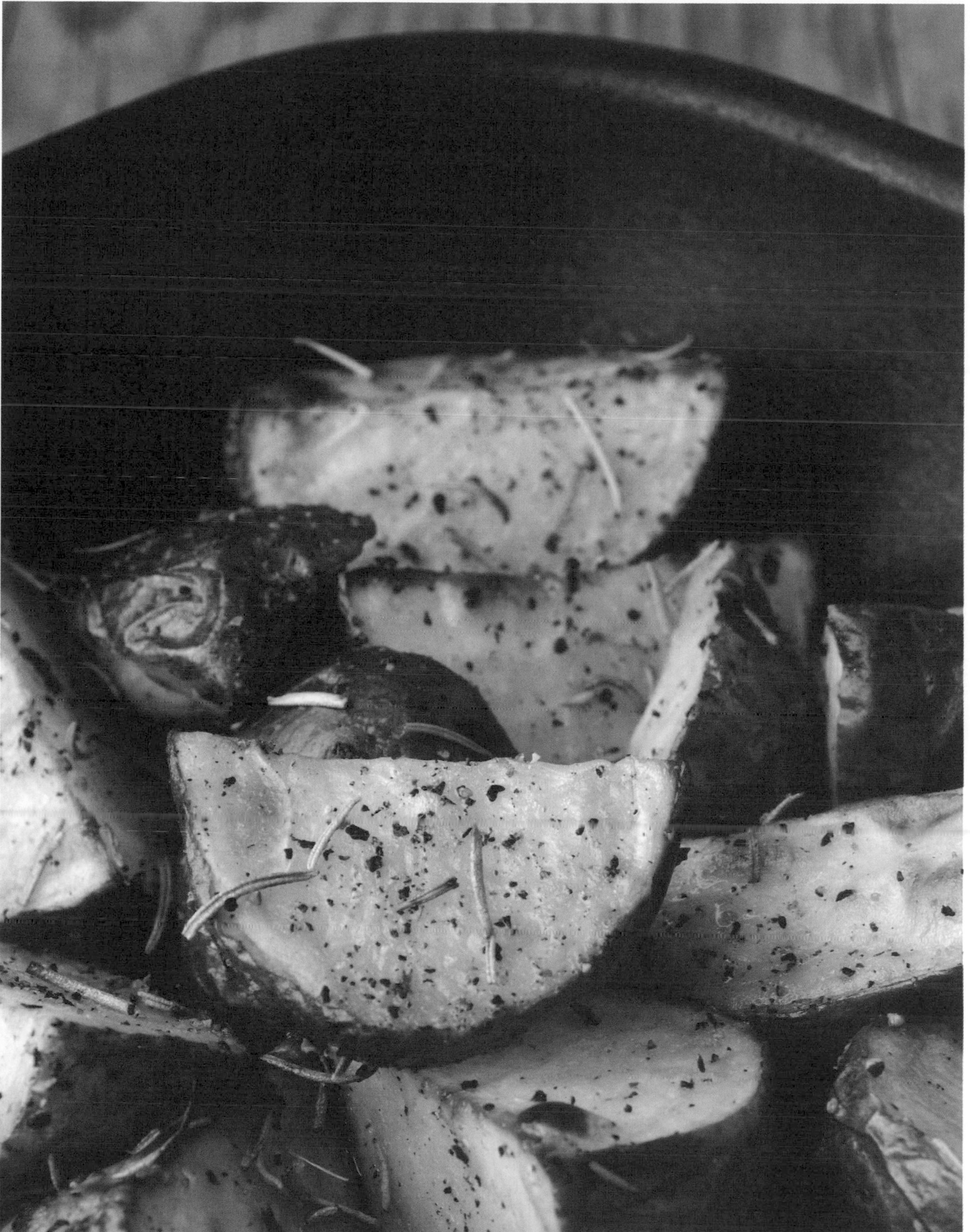

MARVELOUS MUSHROOMS

SERVES 4 ✦ ACTIVE TIME: 20 MINUTES ✦ START TO FINISH: 30 MINUTES

Sautéing mushrooms in the skillet with lots of butter yields a rich, earthy stew that is delicious with steak and potatoes. Or serve these mushrooms as a topping for burgers or even baked polenta with cheese.

6 tablespoons butter, cut into pieces

1 pound mushrooms, cut into slices

1 teaspoon Vermouth

Salt and pepper to taste

1. Heat the skillet over medium-high heat. Add the butter. When melted, add the mushrooms. Cook, stirring, until the mushrooms begin to soften, about 5 minutes. Reduce the heat to low and let the mushrooms simmer, stirring occasionally, until they cook down, about 15 to 20 minutes.
2. Add the Vermouth and stir, then season with salt and pepper. Allow to simmer until the mushrooms practically melt in your mouth. Serve hot.

There are many kinds of mushrooms available, and you can mix and match them as you desire. But my favorite to use with this dish is the basic white mushroom.

POLENTA CAKES WITH GREENS

MAKES 4 TO 6 SERVINGS ✦ ACTIVE TIME: 30 MINUTES ✦ START TO FINISH: 60 MINUTES

Polenta is cornmeal cooked into a porridge and then baked or fried. It forms a lovely, bright yellow cake that is moist yet firm. It can be topped with all kinds of things, but in this recipe, it is the base for sauteed vegetables. Delicious!

Olive oil for preparing skillet

1 cup coarse-grind or medium-grind polenta

3 cups water

Salt and freshly ground black pepper

1 pounds bitter greens such as kale, chard, escarole, or dandelion, tough stems removed

3 tablespoons extra virgin olive oil

3 cloves garlic, chopped

Red pepper flakes

Grated Romano for topping

1. Preheat the oven to 400 degrees.
2. Liberally oil the skillet and put it in the oven for a few minutes to heat.
3. In a heavy saucepan, whisk together the polenta and water. Heat over medium and bring to a boil, whisking to prevent lumps from forming. When bubbling, reduce the heat to low and simmer, uncovered, for a couple of minutes or until smooth. Season with salt and black pepper.
4. Pour the polenta into the skillet. Put in the oven and bake for about 30 minutes, until it is lightly golden and coming away from the edges of the pan.
5. While it's baking, make the greens. Bring a large pot of salted water to a boil, add the greens, and boil until very tender, 15 to 20 minutes. Drain in a colander and squeeze to remove excess moisture. Cut the greens into pieces. Heat the olive oil in a pan, add the garlic and cook, stirring, until fragrant, about 2 minutes. Add the red pepper flakes, stir, then add the greens. Cook until heated through. Season with salt and pepper. Keep warm until polenta is cooked.
6. Cut the polenta into wedges, top with the greens, and sprinkle on the grated cheese.

QUINOA SKILLET CASSEROLE

SERVES 6 ✦ ACTIVE TIME: 30 MINUTES ✦ START TO FINISH: 60 MINUTES

There are lots of health benefits of quinoa, but one of the drawbacks of this nutritious food is that it can cook up sticky, like oatmeal—a texture that isn't always appealing. With the cast-iron skillet, you can cook the quinoa so that it gets almost crackly-crunchy. Combined with the veggies and hot peppers, this is a delish dish.

1 cup dry quinoa

2 cups chicken broth

1½ tablespoons olive oil

1 ear of cooked corn, kernels removed

½ red bell pepper, diced

½ cup onion, chopped

1 jalapeno, seeded and sliced

½ teaspoon salt

1 cup cheddar cheese, grated

1. In a small saucepan with a tight-fitting lid, cook the quinoa in the broth. Bring the liquid to a boil, stir, and reduce the heat to low, simmering for about 15 minutes or until grains are translucent. Remove from heat and let sit, covered, for at least 5 more minutes so it fully absorbs the broth.
2. Heat the skillet over medium-high heat, add the olive oil, and then add the corn, red pepper, onion, and jalapeno slices. Stir, cooking, until onion is softened and peppers are starting to brown, about 5 to 8 minutes.
3. Stir in the quinoa, season with salt, and combine all the ingredients. Keep the skillet on medium-high to brown the quinoa somewhat.
4. Cook for another 10 minutes, stirring occasionally. Stir in the cheese, remove from heat, and serve.

Quinoa looks and cooks like a grain, but it's actually a seed—the harvest from a grass called goosefoot that has grown in the Andes Mountains of South America for millennia. It's high in protein and fiber and loaded with magnesium, iron, and B6.

ONE-POT MAC-AND-CHEESE

MAKES 6 TO 8 SERVINGS **ACTIVE TIME: 30 MINUTES** **START TO FINISH: 60 MINUTES**

There's nothing like homemade macaroni and cheese, but it can get as messy to make as it is to eat when you have to use several pots and pans to make and serve it. Here comes your cast-iron skillet to the rescue!

1 pound elbow macaroni (uncooked)

1 tablespoon salt

3 tablespoons butter, room temperature

3½ tablespoons flour

1½ cups milk, room temperature or slightly warmed

¼ cup sour cream

¾ pound sharp white cheddar, grated

¼ pound Gruyère cheese, grated

Salt and pepper to taste

Dash of cayenne pepper

Preheat the oven to 425 degrees.

Put the macaroni in the skillet and add cold water so that it reaches ¼ inch below the top. Stir in the salt, turn the heat on to high, and cook the macaroni as the water boils for about 10 minutes. Test a piece after about 7 minutes. The pasta should be al dente—nearly cooked through but still a bit chewy. When it is cooked like this, drain it in a colander over a large mixing bowl so the water is retained.

Put your skillet back on the stove over medium heat, and add the butter. When it's melted, stir in the flour with a wooden spoon if possible, stirring constantly so no lumps form. When it is starting to bubble, start adding the milk, whisking constantly as you add it slowly. Add about a half cup at a time, being sure to whisk it thoroughly before continuing. When all the milk is stirred in, let the sauce simmer over low heat for about 10 minutes until thickened.

On low to medium heat, stir in the sour cream. When the mix is warm again, stir in the cheeses, stirring gently as they melt. Season with the salt, pepper, and cayenne.

Finally, add the macaroni gently into the cheese sauce. If it seems too thick, add some of the macaroni water. The consistency should be like a thick stew. When the noodles are hot, transfer the skillet to the oven.

Bake in the oven for about 15 minutes, then take a peek. The dish should be bubbling and the cheese on the top starting to brown. This takes somewhere between 15 and 25 minutes. Be careful not to let it burn. Let the macaroni cool slightly before serving.

Macaroni and cheese is a dish that's great fun to personalize. There are all sorts of ways you can change it up a bit. Try using different amounts of different cheeses (but always those that melt well, which are typically hard cheeses or aged cheeses); add bacon bits; add chopped (seeded) tomatoes; add chopped green onions; add jalapeno peppers; sprinkle bread crumbs on top for a crunchy layer; or try using different pasta shapes like mini penne, orichietti, or even pinwheels.

SAUTEED GREENS

MAKES 4 TO 6 SERVINGS ✦ ACTIVE TIME: 20 MINUTES ✦ START TO FINISH: 30 MINUTES

When you first pile the greens into the skillet, you may think you're using the wrong pan, as they will overflow. But the greens cook down significantly, and in the end it will all be beautiful.

2 tablespoons olive oil

2 cloves garlic, sliced thin

½ teaspoon red pepper flakes

One bunch Swiss chard, tough ends removed, leaves chopped

One bunch kale, tough stems removed, leaves chopped

Salt and pepper to taste

1. Heat the oil in the skillet over medium-high heat. Add the garlic. Cook until garlic is "dancing" in the oil, 1 to 2 minutes. Add the red pepper flakes.
2. Add the greens, stirring gently to expose all of them to the hot oil. Reduce the heat to medium and continue to gently stir in large scoops as the greens cook down.
3. When the greens aren't overflowing the skillet, allow them to cook over medium heat for 5 to 10 minutes, stirring only occasionally, until wilted and soft. Add more oil to keep the pan from drying out if necessary.
4. When soft and cooked down, transfer to a bowl, season with salt and pepper, and serve.

HOME-STYLE BAKED BEANS

MAKES 6 TO 8 SERVINGS ✦ ACTIVE TIME: 30 MINUTES ✦ START TO FINISH: 1½ TO 2 HOURS

I still have the picture in my head of cowboys cooking in a cast iron skillet over an open fire while their horses hang out behind them. What are they eating? In my mind, it's baked beans with bacon, which seems quintessentially "skillet cooking" to me. So here's a recipe in honor of my vision.

6 strips thick-cut bacon, divided in half

½ onion, diced

½ cup diced bell pepper (ribs and seeds removed)

1 teaspoon salt

2 (15.5-oz.) cans pinto beans, rinsed and drained

1 cup barbecue sauce (not too sweet!)

1 teaspoon Dijon mustard

2 tablespoons dark brown sugar

Fresh ground pepper

1. Preheat the oven to 325 degrees.
2. Heat the skillet over medium heat and cook half the bacon pieces. Cook until it's just soft, about 8 minutes. Transfer to a plate lined with paper towels to drain.
3. In the fat, add the remaining pieces of bacon, turn up the heat, and cook, flipping often, until pieces are browned. Reduce the heat to medium. Add the onion and pepper and cook, stirring occasionally, until the vegetables soften, another 8 minutes or so.
4. Add the salt, beans, barbecue sauce, mustard, and brown sugar. Stir, season with additional salt and a generous grind of fresh pepper, and leave on the stove until the liquid just starts to simmer.
5. Lay the partially cooked pieces of bacon on top and transfer the skillet to the oven.
6. Bake for 1 hour and take a look. The bacon should be crisp and browned, and the beans should be thick. This can go for another 15 to 30 minutes more if the consistency isn't right. Just be careful not to overcook them, in which case the beans will start to dry out. An hour and 15 to 20 minutes is about right.
7. Remove from the oven and allow to cool slightly before serving, preferably in bowls around a fire!

Baked beans are delicious and filling on their own, but they are the perfect accompaniment to grilled sausages, hot dogs, hamburgers, pork chops, or barbecued chicken. Their thickness is also complemented by cole slaw or a big green salad. Cornbread (page 176) makes the meal.

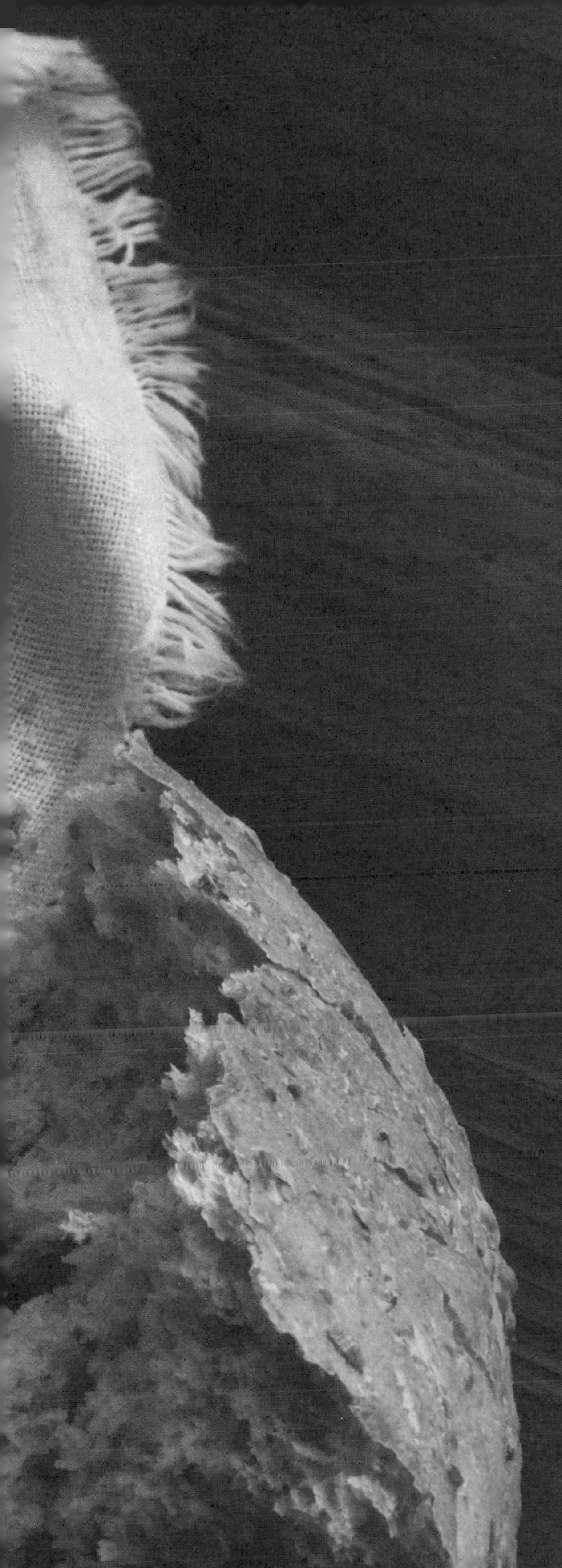

BREADS

Wait until you taste the mouth-watering breads that will be coming out of your oven when you start baking with the cast-iron skillet! You'll find that things are cooked more evenly, yielding the best-tasting breads, buns, flatbreads, and more. This chapter includes some basic breads, such as biscuits, dinner rolls, and cornbread, that are sure to be family favorites. Because grain-based breads have been cooked over fires since our earliest days, this chapter includes recipes for breads made around the world, like naan from India, soda bread from Ireland, focaccia from Italy, and even Ethiopian injera. For these recipes, either a 12.5" skillet or slightly larger will do the job.

CORNBREAD

SERVES 6 TO 8 ✦ ACTIVE TIME: 20 MINUTES ✦ START TO FINISH: 60 MINUTES

If you're going to make bread in a cast-iron skillet, you have to make cornbread! Many restaurants serve cornbread in a cast-iron skillet, which adds something to the flavor, if you ask me. No matter how you serve it, it tastes great.

2 cups finely ground yellow cornmeal

1 cup flour

¼ cup sugar

2 teaspoons baking powder

1 teaspoon baking soda

1 teaspoon salt

5 tablespoons unsalted butter, divided

1½ cups milk

2 eggs

1. Preheat the oven to 400 degrees.
2. In a large bowl, combine cornmeal, flour, sugar, baking powder, baking soda, and salt. Put ½ cup milk in a measuring cup. Add 2 tablespoons butter, cut into pieces. Put in the microwave and heat on high for 1 minute so that butter is melted into the milk. Pour this over the dry ingredients and begin stirring. Gradually add the additional cup of milk and stir, then add the eggs and continue stirring until thoroughly combined.
3. Heat the skillet over medium heat and melt the 3 remaining tablespoons of butter in it. Add the batter and shake the pan gently to evenly distribute.
4. Transfer the skillet to the oven and cook for 25 to 30 minutes, until light golden brown and a toothpick inserted in the middle comes out clean.
5. Using pot holders or oven mitts, remove the skillet from the oven and let the bread cool for 10 to 15 minutes before slicing and serving.

Cornbread recipes are as varied and plentiful as those for chili. A great way to discover different ones that you like without having to go through multiple cookbooks and lots of time in the kitchen yourself is to invite friends and family to a Cast-Iron Cornbread Cook-Off. Make the chili the way you like it (and plenty of it), then have people bring over their cornbreads with recipes.

CORNY-SPICY BREAD

SERVES 6 TO 8 ✦ ACTIVE TIME: 25 MINUTES ✦ START TO FINISH: 60 MINUTES

Now that I've suggested the family or neighborhood cornbread challenge, I have to offer my own contender for first prize, since I love a cornbread that actually has kernels of corn in it. If you like spicy, toss in the jalapeños, too.

2 cups finely ground yellow cornmeal

1 cup flour

¼ cup sugar

2 teaspoons baking powder

1 teaspoon baking soda

1 teaspoon salt

4 tablespoons unsalted butter, divided

1½ cups milk

2 eggs

1 cup corn kernels (can be from fresh-cooked corn on the cob, or use canned being sure to drain the liquid)

¼ to ½ cup diced jalapeño peppers

1. Preheat the oven to 400 degrees.
2. In a large bowl, combine the cornmeal, flour, sugar, baking powder, baking soda, and salt. Put ½ cup milk in a measuring cup. Add the 2 tablespoons butter, cut into pieces. Put in the microwave and heat on high for 1 minute so that butter is melted into the milk. Pour this over the dry ingredients and begin stirring. Gradually add the additional cup of milk and stir, then add the eggs and continue stirring until thoroughly combined. When batter is mixed, fold in the corn kernels and jalapeños.
3. Heat the skillet over medium heat and melt the 2 remaining tablespoons of butter in it. Add the batter and shake the pan gently to evenly distribute.
4. Transfer the skillet to the oven and cook for 25 to 30 minutes, until light golden brown and a toothpick inserted in the middle comes out clean.
5. Using pot holders or oven mitts, remove the skillet from the oven and let the bread cool for 10 to 15 minutes before slicing and serving.

DINNER ROLLS

MAKES ABOUT A DOZEN ROLLS ✦ ACTIVE TIME: 1 HOUR ✦ START TO FINISH: 3 HOURS

These classic dinner rolls are light, flaky, and buttery perfection.

1¼ cups whole milk, heated to 110 degrees

3 tablespoons sugar

1 tablespoon active dry yeast

8 tablespoons (1 stick) unsalted butter

¾ teaspoon salt

2 eggs at room temperature, lightly beaten

3½ cups cake or bread flour (not all-purpose flour)

1. In a small bowl, combine ½ cup warm milk and the sugar. Sprinkle the yeast over it, stir, and set aside so the yeast can proof (about 10 minutes).
2. While the yeast is proofing, melt the butter in the skillet over low to medium heat, and remove from heat when melted.
3. When the yeast mix is frothy, stir in 3 tablespoons of the melted butter, the remaining milk, the salt, and the eggs. Then stir in the flour, mixing until all ingredients are incorporated. Transfer to a lightly floured surface and knead the dough for 5 to 10 minutes until it is soft and springy and elastic.
4. Coat the bottom and sides of a large mixing bowl (ceramic is best) with butter. Place the ball of dough in the bowl, cover loosely with plastic wrap, put it in a naturally warm, draft-free location, and let it rise until doubled in size, about 45 minutes to 1 hour.
5. Prepare a lightly floured surface to work on. Punch down the dough in the bowl and transfer it to the floured surface. Warm the skillet with the butter so that it is melted again.
6. Break off pieces of the dough to form into rolls, shaping them into 2-inch balls with your hands. Roll the balls in the butter in the skillet, and leave them in the skillet as they're made and buttered.
7. Cover the skillet loosely with a clean dish towel, put it in the warm, draft-free spot, and let the rolls rise until doubled in size, about 30 minutes. While they're rising, preheat the oven to 350 degrees.
8. When the rolls have risen and the oven is ready, cover the skillet with aluminum foil and bake in the oven for 20 minutes. Remove the foil and finish cooking, another 15 minutes or so, until the rolls are golden on top and light and springy. Serve warm.

It's important to proof the yeast before adding it to your recipe to ensure that it is fresh and active. If it is, it reacts with the sugar and liquid and creates tiny bubbles. It also releases a smell that is described (appropriately enough) as "yeasty"—the smell you get from fresh-baked bread. Yeast reacts with sugar to release carbon dioxide and, eventually, alcohol. This is the basis of making beer and wine, too. But with baking, the fermentation process stops when the live cells are cooked in the oven.

Cast-iron skillets are created by the centuries-old process of pouring molten iron into a sand mold. When the skillet has cooled, the mold is broken apart, and the skillet—along with its handle—is removed fully intact. It's this time-tested durability that makes stovetop-to-oven recipes possible with your skillet.

BISCUITS

SERVES 4 TO 6 ✦ ACTIVE TIME: 20 MINUTES ✦ START TO FINISH: 40 MINUTES

For fluffy biscuits, you need to work with a very hot skillet. The golden brown crust on the bottom is as much of a delight as the airy, warm dough.

2 cups flour

1 teaspoon sugar

1 teaspoon salt

1 tablespoon baking powder

6 to 8 tablespoons butter, cut into pieces

½ cup + 2 tablespoons buttermilk

1. Preheat oven to 450 degrees.
2. In a large bowl, combine the flour, sugar, salt, and baking powder.
3. Using a fork or pastry knife, blend in 6 tablespoons of the butter to form crumbly dough. Form a well in the middle and add ½ cup buttermilk. Stir to combine and form a stiff dough. Using your fingers works best! If it seems too dry, add 1 tablespoon more of the buttermilk, going to 2 tablespoons if necessary.
4. Put 2 tablespoons butter in the skillet and put it in the oven to melt while the skillet heats.
5. Put the dough on a lightly floured surface and press out to a thickness of about 1 inch. Press out biscuits using an inverted water glass. Place the biscuits in the skillet and bake for about 10 minutes, until golden on the bottom.

Biscuits are another buttery bread that can be served with savory or sweet additions. You can make mini ham sandwiches by splitting the biscuits, putting some mayonnaise and grainy mustard on them, and putting in a slice of fresh-baked ham. You can fill them with scrambled eggs and bacon bits. Or you can slather them with butter and your favorite jam or honey. Or just eat them as-is.

CREPES

MAKES 8 TO 10 SERVINGS (ABOUT 16 CREPES) ✦ ACTIVE TIME: 1 HOUR ✦ START TO FINISH: 6 HOURS

These are very thin pancakes that can be filled with any number of things. The batter can be made with or without sugar, depending on whether you want to fill them with savory or sweet ingredients. Making them for the first time is intimidating, as it involves getting a hang of the right amount of batter on the skillet that's heated to the right temperature, but once you get the hang of it, it's a very satisfying experience that yields great results!

4 tablespoons melted butter

3 eggs

⅛ teaspoon salt

1 cup whole milk (possibly more)

1 cup flour (minus 2 tablespoons)

1. Heat the skillet over low heat to melt 2 tablespoons of the butter very slowly.
2. In a large mixing bowl, whisk the eggs until smooth. Add the salt and milk and whisk together until well blended. Whisk in the flour and, while whisking, add 2 tablespoons of the melted butter. Keep whisking until the batter is smooth and there are no lumps. Cover the bowl with plastic wrap or a clean dish towel, put in a cool, dark place, and let rest for 3 or 4 hours before making the crepes.
3. You'll need a spatula that won't scratch the surface of the skillet. Have that and a ladle for scooping out the batter ready by the stove.
4. Heat the skillet over medium-high heat and melt a slice of the remaining 2 tablespoons of butter in it. Stir the crepe batter to blend again. When the skillet is hot but not smoking (the butter should not brown), use the ladle to scoop about ¼ cup into the skillet. When the batter hits the pan, tilt it gently to spread the batter evenly over the bottom. When the bottom is covered, cook for just over 1 minute and then flip the crepe over and cook the other side for about half the time. Tilt the skillet over a plate to slide the crepe out.
5. You should be able to make several crepes per slice of butter, but gauge the pan by how dry it is, and if you think it needs butter, add some. If the pan gets too hot and the butter browns, wipe it out with a paper towel and start over.
6. Continue making the crepes until all the batter is used up. As they cool on the plate, put pieces of waxed paper between them to keep them from sticking together. If you're not going to use them right away, wrap the stack in aluminum foil and keep them in the refrigerator or freeze them.

Variations

- To make dessert crepes, add 3 tablespoons of sugar when you add the flour, and 2 tablespoons Cognac (or 1 tablespoon vanilla) once the batter is mixed.
- Fill savory crepes with a variety of cooked meats, poultry, or fish, in a sauce. For example, you can use pieces of leftover chicken in a cream sauce with peas and mushrooms. Roll a generous spoonful up in the crepe, tuck it into a baking dish (with others), sprinkle with shredded cheese and bake in the oven at 350 degrees for about 10 minutes.
- Cook some spicy Italian sausage, spread some ricotta on the crepe, add the sausage, season with salt and pepper, roll up and put in a baking dish, cover with marinara and shredded mozzarella, and bake at 350 degrees for about 15 minutes.

NAAN

MAKES 4 TO 8 SERVINGS (8 PIECES) ✦ ACTIVE TIME: 1 HOUR ✦ START TO FINISH: 3 TO 4 HOURS

This is the bread that is traditionally served with Indian cuisine, from spicy to saucy. It's cooked in a tandoor (clay oven) in India, but the cast-iron skillet turns out a very good replication!

1½ teaspoons active dry yeast

½ tablespoon sugar

1 cup warm water (110 to 115 degrees)

3 cups all-purpose flour or 1½ cups all-purpose and 1½ cups whole wheat pastry flour

¼ teaspoon salt

1 teaspoon baking powder

½ cup plain yogurt

4 tablespoons unsalted butter

¼ cup olive oil

1. Proof the yeast by mixing it with the sugar and ½ cup of the warm water. Let sit for 10 minutes until foamy.
2. In a bowl, combine the flour, salt, baking powder, remaining water, and yeast mix. Stir to combine well. Add the yogurt and 2 tablespoons of the butter, melted, and stir to form a soft dough.
3. Transfer to a lightly floured surface and knead the dough until it is springy and elastic, about 10 minutes.
4. Grease the inside of a large bowl (preferably ceramic) with butter, and put the dough inside, turning to coat on all sides. Cover with plastic wrap or a clean dish cloth, put in a warm, draft-free place, and allow to rise, 1 hour or more, until doubled in bulk.
5. Punch down the dough. Lightly flour a work surface again, take out the dough and, using a rolling pin, make a circle with the dough and cut it into 8 slices (like a pie).
6. Heat the skillet over high heat until it is very hot (about 5 minutes). Working with individual pieces of dough, roll them out to soften the sharp edges and make the pieces look more like teardrops. Brush both sides with olive oil and, working one at a time, place the pieces in the skillet.
7. Cook for 1 minute, turn the dough with tongs, cover the skillet, and cook the other side for about a minute (no longer). Transfer cooked naan to a plate and cover with foil to keep warm while making the additional pieces. Serve warm.

Variations

You can add herbs or spices to the dough or the pan to make naan with different flavors.

- Add ¼ cup chopped fresh parsley to the dough.
- Sprinkle the skillet lightly with cumin or coriander or turmeric (or a combination) before cooking the pieces of naan.
- Use a seasoned olive oil to brush the pieces before cooking—one with hot pepper flakes or roasted garlic.

FOCACCIA

SERVES 4 TO 6 ✦ ACTIVE TIME: 90 MINUTES ✦ START TO FINISH: 3 HOURS

This is essentially a raised flatbread—like a crustier pizza—to which all kinds of yummy things can be added. It's become synonymous with Italian cuisine, and it's certainly popular in Italy, but it's also made throughout the Mediterranean countries, from Istria through southern France. You can find it in grocery stores, but there's nothing like a fresh piece right out of the skillet, still warm, with toppings just the way you want them. This one is a simple salt/Parmesan focaccia.

1 packet active dry yeast (2¼ teaspoons)

2 cups water (110 to 115 degrees)

4 to 4½ cups flour

2 teaspoons salt

3 tablespoons olive oil, plus more for drizzling over bread before baking

Sea salt (coarse grained) and freshly ground black pepper

Grated Parmesan for topping

1. Proof the yeast by mixing it with the warm water. Let sit for 10 minutes until foamy.
2. In a bowl, combine the flour, salt, and yeast mix. Stir to combine well. Transfer to a lightly floured surface and knead the dough until it loses its stickiness, adding more flour as needed, about 10 minutes.
3. Coat the bottom and sides of a large mixing bowl (ceramic is best) with olive oil. Place the ball of dough in the bowl, cover loosely with plastic wrap, put it in a naturally warm, draft-free location, and let it rise until doubled in size, about 45 minutes to 1 hour.
4. Preheat the oven to 450 degrees.
5. When risen, turn the dough out onto a lightly floured surface and divide it in half. Put a tablespoon of olive oil in the skillet, and press one of the pieces of dough into it. Drizzle some olive oil over it and sprinkle with salt and pepper, then with Parmesan cheese. Cover loosely with plastic wrap and let rise for about 20 minutes. With the other piece, press it out onto a piece of parchment paper and follow the same procedure to top it and let it rise.
6. Put in the middle of the oven and bake for 25 to 30 minutes until golden and hot. Remove from oven and let rest for 5 minutes before removing from skillet to cool further. Wipe any crumbs off the skillet, coat with some more olive oil, and transfer the other round to the skillet. Bake for about 25 minutes.
7. If desired, you can put the extra dough in a plastic bag and store it in the refrigerator for up to 3 days to use later.

TORTILLAS

MAKES 6 TO 12 SERVINGS (12 LARGE TORTILLAS) ✦ ACTIVE TIME: 30 MINUTES ✦ START TO FINISH: 50 TO 60 MINUTES

We are covering flatbreads from around the world, so now, on to Mexico! These are even simpler to make than the ones that involved yeast. There's no need to let the dough rise for tortillas—simply mix, knead, and shape—all with your hands, which is really fun. Then cook. Oh, and eat!

3 cups flour

1 teaspoon salt

2 teaspoons baking powder

3 tablespoons Crisco shortening (or 4 tablespoons chilled butter)

1½ cups water at room temperature

1. Put the flour in a large bowl. Mix in the salt and baking powder.
2. Add the shortening (or butter), and using your fingers, blend it into the flour mix until you have a crumbly dough. Add 1 cup of the water and work it in, then portions of the additional half cup, working it in with your hands, so that you create a dough that's not too sticky.
3. Lightly flour a work surface and turn out the dough. Knead it for about 10 minutes until it's soft and elastic. Divide it into 12 equal pieces.
4. Using a lightly floured rolling pin, roll each piece out to almost the size of the bottom of the skillet.
5. Heat the skillet over high heat. Add a tortilla. Cook for just 15 seconds a side, flipping to cook both sides. Keep the cooked tortillas warm by putting them on a plate covered with a damp tea towel. Serve warm.

A homemade tortilla begs for a filling of sliced, grilled meat with shredded cheese, chopped tomatoes, chopped red onions, chopped lettuce, and sliced jalapenos.

PITA BREAD

MAKES 16 PITAS ✦ ACTIVE TIME: 1 HOUR ✦ START TO FINISH: 2 HOURS

*And here's an easy recipe for another flatbread that originated in the Mediterranean region, purportedly ancient Greece, as the word itself is Greek—*pektos*—meaning solid or clotted. It is popular around the world but especially in Middle Eastern countries.*

1 envelope active dry yeast

2½ cups water (110 to 115 degrees)

3 cups flour

1 tablespoon olive oil

1 tablespoon salt

3 cups whole wheat flour

1. Proof the yeast by mixing with the warm water. Let sit for about 10 minutes until foamy.
2. In a large bowl, add the yeast mix into the regular flour and stir until it forms a stiff dough. Cover and let the dough rise for about 1 hour.
3. Add the oil and salt to the dough and stir in the whole wheat flour in ½-cup increments. When finished, the dough should be soft. Turn onto a lightly floured surface and knead it until it is smooth and elastic, about 10 minutes.
4. Lightly grease a large bowl, put the dough in, turn to cover all sides, put a clean dish towel over the top and let it sit in a warm, draft-free spot for at least 1 hour, until doubled in size.
5. On a lightly floured surface, punch down the dough and cut into 16 pieces. Put the pieces on a baking sheet and cover with a dish towel while working with individual pieces.
6. Roll out the pieces with a rolling pin until they are approximately 7 inches across. Stack them between sheets of plastic wrap.
7. Heat the skillet over high heat and lightly oil the bottom. Cook the individual pitas about 20 seconds on one side, then flip and cook for about a minute on the other side, until bubbles form. Turn again and continue to cook until the pita puffs up, another minute or so. Keep the skillet lightly oiled while processing, and store the pitas on a plate under a clean dish towel until ready to serve.

Pitas make delicious, somewhat chewy bread pockets that can be filled with just about anything. In summer, I like to smear the inside with fresh hummus and top with chopped carrots, lettuce, tomatoes, and hot sauce. Make a grilled cheese sandwich by putting some butter, slices of Swiss cheese, slices of American cheese, and slices of tomatoes inside, wrapping the sandwich in foil, heating it inside the foil on the skillet or on a grill for about 5 minutes a side, then unwrapping it and lightly toasting it directly on the hot pan.

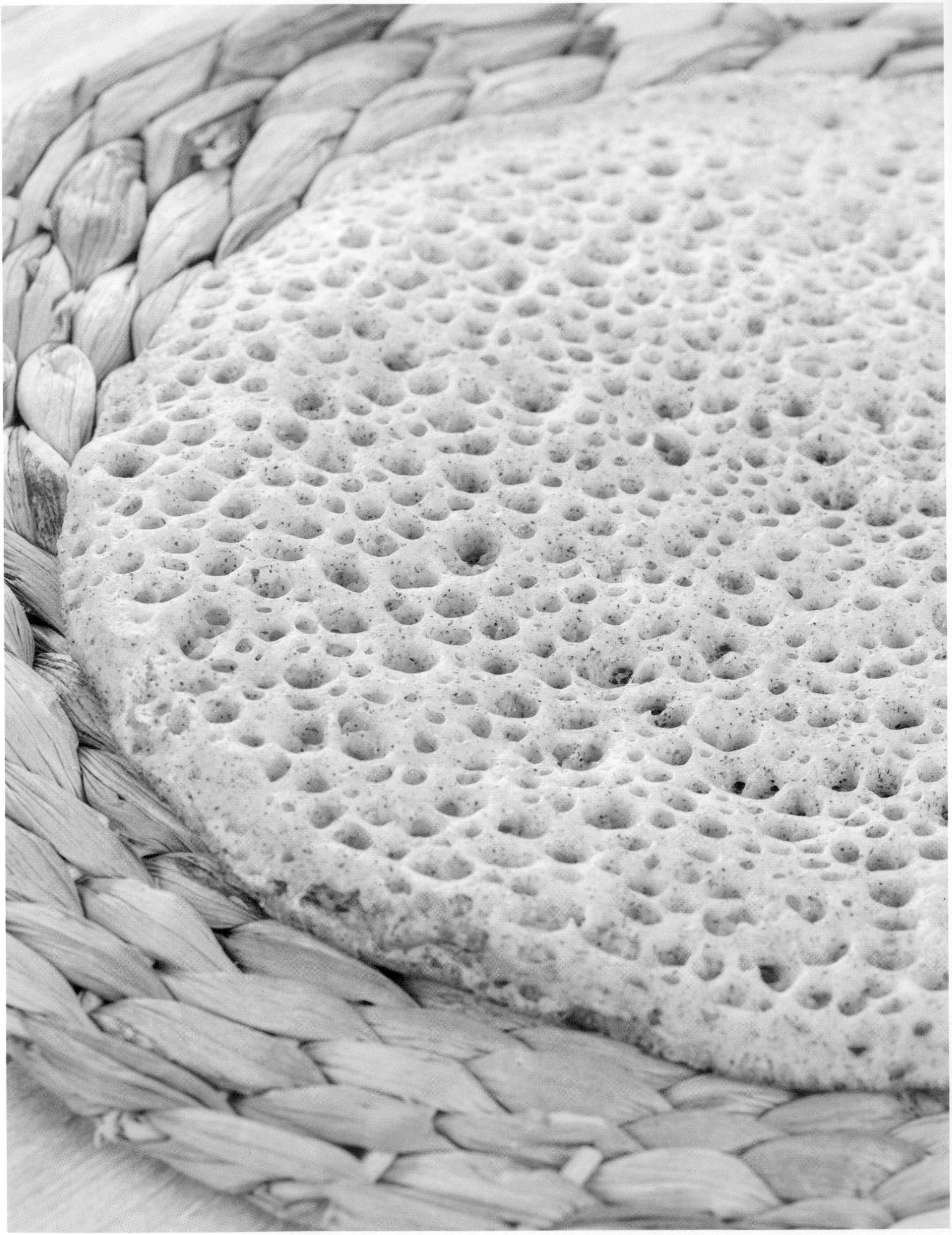

ETHIOPIAN INJERA

MAKES 1 INJERA ✦ ACTIVE TIME: 1 HOUR ✦ START TO FINISH: 3 DAYS

If you've ever eaten at an Ethiopian restaurant, you'll remember that the centerpiece of the meal is the thick, spongy bread that's placed in the middle of the table. The dishes go around it, and you eat by ripping apart the bread and scooping up the other foods. I like to use it as almost a polenta or spongy pizza crust, topping with whatever leftovers I can combine to taste good. While the ingredients are minimal, you have to plan ahead for the day you want to serve the injera, as the "flour" needs to sit for several days to break down the grain.

½ teaspoon active dry yeast

2 cups water (110 to 115 degrees)

1½ cups ground teff (put the seeds in a food processor or blender to reduce to "flour")

Salt

Vegetable oil

1. Stir the yeast in with the water and let it proof for about 10 minutes.
2. Put the ground teff in a bowl and add the water/yeast. Mix thoroughly until a stiff dough forms. Put a dish towel over the bowl and stick it in a draft-free, fairly warm place in your kitchen. Let it sit for several days. It will bubble and turn brown and smell sour. Let it sit for 2 to 3 days.
3. When ready to make the injera, add salt to the mix until some of the sour "bite" has dissipated. The mix at this time should resemble pancake batter.
4. Heat the skillet over medium heat and brush with vegetable oil. Pour enough batter on the pan to coat the bottom less than a pancake but more than a crepe. Tilt to spread the batter over the bottom of the skillet. Cook until holes form in the bread and the edges crisp up and lift away from the pan. The bread should not be flipped so be sure to let it cook thoroughly.
5. When cooked, lift it out with a spatula and put it on a plate or platter to cool. Place plastic wrap between injeras as you cook a batch of them. Serve warm with bowls of things like sautéed vegetables, grilled meat pieces, creamed spinach, sautéed mushrooms, or authentic Ethiopian dishes you can make—or Indian dishes you can find in grocery stores.

Thank goodness for Bob's Red Mill. They are bringing exotic grains from around the world to grocery stores here in the United States. One of those grains is teff, a wheat-like grain that's cultivated almost exclusively in Ethiopia. Teff is the smallest grain in the world, and it looks almost like poppy seeds (100 teff grains equal the size of a kernel of wheat!). It's full of iron, and it's gluten free. Bob's Red Mill website has recipes for teff, so you won't have to use the bag just to make injera—unless you want to.

PEPPERONI BREAD

MAKES 6 TO 8 SERVINGS ✦ ACTIVE TIME: 1 HOUR ✦ START TO FINISH: 3 HOURS

This is a favorite during football season, when the game hasn't actually started until this makes an appearance in front of the TV. Start in the morning for an afternoon game, as the dough needs to rise several times. But it's so delicious!

1¼ cups water (110 to 115 degrees)

1 oz. active dry yeast

1 tablespoon melted butter

1 ½ teaspoons salt

3½ cups flour

Salt and pepper

½ pound pepperoni, slivered

2 cups grated mozzarella cheese

1 teaspoon hot pepper flakes

1 teaspoon dried oregano

1 teaspoon garlic powder

1 tablespoon sugar

1. Proof the yeast by mixing the water and sugar in a large bowl and then adding the yeast, stirring. Let sit until foamy, about 10 minutes. Add the salt and about half the flour to form a sticky dough. Cover the bowl with plastic wrap or a clean dish towel and let rise in a warm, draft-free place until it is double in size, about 1 hour.
2. Punch down the dough and add more flour to make it less sticky. Transfer to a floured surface and work the dough until it's smooth and elastic. Transfer to a lightly greased bowl and let sit for about 15 minutes.
3. On the floured surface, roll the dough out into a rectangle about 14x16 inches. Sprinkle with salt and pepper, spread the dough with pieces of pepperoni, then cheese, and top with a sprinkling of hot pepper flakes, oregano, and garlic powder. Roll up like a jellyroll, pinching the ends to secure filling.
4. Grease the skillet with the butter and lay the roll in it in a circle, working from the edges toward the center. Cover with a clean dish towel and let it rise again for about 1 hour. Preheat the oven to 375 degrees.
5. Bake the pepperoni bread for about 30 minutes, until golden on top and bubbling in the center. Serve immediately.

This dish is like a deluxe calzone: pizza dough folded over filling. Go ahead and fill with whatever you typically like on a pizza—mushrooms, spinach, ricotta cheese, sausage, barbequed chicken, pineapple and ham—even anchovies if your family approves. Touchdown!

GARLIC ROSEMARY ROLLS

MAKES 6 TO 8 SERVINGS (8 ROLLS) ✦ ACTIVE TIME: 1.5 HOURS ✦ START TO FINISH: 3 HOURS

These fragrant rolls are a welcome addition to everything from spaghetti and meatballs to a roast leg of lamb. Eat them fresh, and freeze the leftovers—if you have any!

1 package active dry yeast

1 cup water (110 to 115 degrees)

1 tablespoon sugar

1 tablespoon butter, melted

1 teaspoon salt

2 cloves garlic, minced

4 cups flour

1 teaspoon fresh rosemary leaves, chopped, or 2 teaspoons dried, crushed rosemary

1 tablespoon butter

1 egg, lightly beaten

Sea salt

1. In a large bowl, mix the yeast, water, and sugar and let the yeast proof for about 10 minutes, until foamy.
2. Next add the melted butter, salt, garlic, and half the flour. Mix until the dough forms a sticky dough. Continue to add flour, mixing to form a soft dough. Add the rosemary with the last addition of flour.
3. Form into a ball, cover the bowl with plastic wrap or a tea towel, put in a warm, draft-free place, and let rise until doubled in size, about 1 hour.
4. Put the skillet in the oven and preheat the oven to 400 degrees.
5. Transfer the dough to a lightly floured surface. Divide into 8 pieces and form into balls.
6. Remove the skillet from the oven and melt the butter in it. Place the rolls in the skillet, turning to cover them with butter. Wash the rolls with the beaten egg and sprinkle with sea salt.
7. Bake in the oven until golden and set, about 40 minutes.

Make cheesy garlic-rosemary rolls by sprinkling Parmesan or pecorino romano cheese on the tops after washing with the beaten egg. Skip the sea salt.

IRISH SODA BREAD

MAKES 1 LOAF ✦ ACTIVE TIME: 30 MINUTES ✦ START TO FINISH: 90 MINUTES

Make this on a weekend morning when you have some extra time, then have slices of it later in the day with a cup of coffee or tea.

4 cups flour

½ cup sugar

⅛ teaspoon salt

3¼ teaspoons baking powder

½ teaspoon baking soda

2 tablespoons caraway seeds

2 large eggs, lightly beaten

1½ cups buttermilk

8 oz. golden raisins

1. Preheat the oven to 450 degrees.
2. Combine the flour, sugar, salt, baking powder, baking soda, and caraway seeds. Add the beaten eggs and stir to combine. Gradually add the buttermilk until the dough is sticky and messy. Stir in the raisins.
3. Generously butter the cast-iron skillet, and scoop and spread the dough in it.
4. Bake for about 1 hour, until the top is crusty and brown and the bread sounds hollow when tapped. Insert a toothpick in the center, too, to be sure the dough is cooked through. It should come out clean.
5. Serve with fresh butter and orange marmalade.

It wouldn't be St. Patrick's Day without Irish Soda bread. According to the Culinary Institute of America, "With a history spanning more than two centuries, soda bread is a traditional Irish specialty. The first loaf, consisting of little more than flour, baking soda, salt, and sour milk, made its debut in the mid-1800s when baking soda found its way into Irish kitchens." They don't mention the raisins or caraway seeds, but I consider these essential!

CHEESY CHIVE SODA BREAD

MAKES 1 LOAF ✦ ACTIVE TIME: 40 MINUTES ✦ START TO FINISH: 90 MINUTES

If you're looking for a savory version of a simple soda bread to serve with something like soup or stew, this is a great recipe.

3 cups white flour

2 cups spelt flour

¾ cup rolled oats (not instant)

2 tablespoons sugar

1 tablespoon baking powder

1 teaspoon salt

1 teaspoon baking soda

8 tablespoons (1 stick) butter, melted and cooled

2½ cups buttermilk

1 large egg, lightly beaten

¼ cup chopped chives

1¼ cups grated sharp white cheddar cheese

Freshly ground pepper

1. Preheat the oven to 350 degrees.
2. In a large bowl, combine the flours, oats, sugar, baking powder, salt, and baking soda. Whisk to combine thoroughly. In another bowl, combine the butter, buttermilk, and egg.
3. Add the milk mixture to the flour mixture and stir vigorously to blend. Dough will be sticky. Stir in the chives and 1 cup of the grated cheese.
4. Liberally grease the skillet with butter. Scoop and spread the dough into the skillet. Grate pepper over the top, then sprinkle the remaining cheese over it. Using a sharp knife, make an "x" in the center, about ½-inch deep, to settle the cheese further into the dough as it cooks.
5. Bake in the oven for about 1 hour and 15 minutes until golden on top and a toothpick inserted in the center comes out clean. Allow to sit in the skillet for a few minutes before serving.

Soda bread doesn't keep so well, so if you happen to have any left over, be sure to wrap it tightly in plastic wrap. Store it in the refrigerator. It will last for about 3 days this way. The bread makes great toast!

YORKSHIRE PUDDING

MAKES 4 TO 6 SERVINGS ✦ ACTIVE TIME: 30 MINUTES ✦ START TO FINISH: 60 MINUTES

This incredible treat is like a savory Dutch baby—a large (and so delicious!) popover. It's traditionally served with roast beef and is, in fact, made with the juices from the meat. Begin your preparation about an hour before the meat will be ready, as the batter needs to sit for a while. My mouth waters just thinking about this classic combination.

1½ cups flour

¾ teaspoon salt

¾ cup milk, room temperature

3 large eggs, room temperature

¾ cup water, room temperature

½ cup beef drippings

1. Preheat the oven to 400 degrees or increase the temperature when you take your roast beef out of the oven.
2. In a large bowl, mix the flour and salt together with a whisk. Make a well in the center of the flour, add the milk and whisk until blended. Next beat the eggs into the batter until thoroughly combined. Add the water, stir this in thoroughly, and set aside for about an hour.
3. When your roast comes out of the oven, pour off ½ cup of drippings and put them in the skillet. Put the skillet in the oven and let the drippings get very hot so that they sizzle. Stir the batter while you're waiting so it's blended. Remove the skillet from the oven, pour the batter in, and return it immediately.
4. Bake for about 30 minutes or until the sides have risen and are gently browned.
5. Bring to the table where the roast beef awaits, and serve with extra juices on the side.

If you want to make this delicious side dish but you're not having roast beef, you can substitute 1/2 cup melted butter for the drippings. Their smoking point is lower than the drippings, so keep an eye on the skillet as it heats up in the oven. The butter will be sizzling before long.

As you may have already discovered with recipes in the other chapters of this book, the cast-iron skillet is remarkably versatile, doing its best "work" going from stovetop to oven, it seems, and being able to render something cooked to crunchy perfection on the outside while retaining a moist center. It might be desserts where this quality is best put to use. Did you know your cast-iron skillet is a pie plate? And a cookie sheet (ok, a small one, but still!)? And a cake pan? Best of all, it is a pan in which you can caramelize butter and sugar and sauté bananas, pears, and apples and other fruits to perfection.

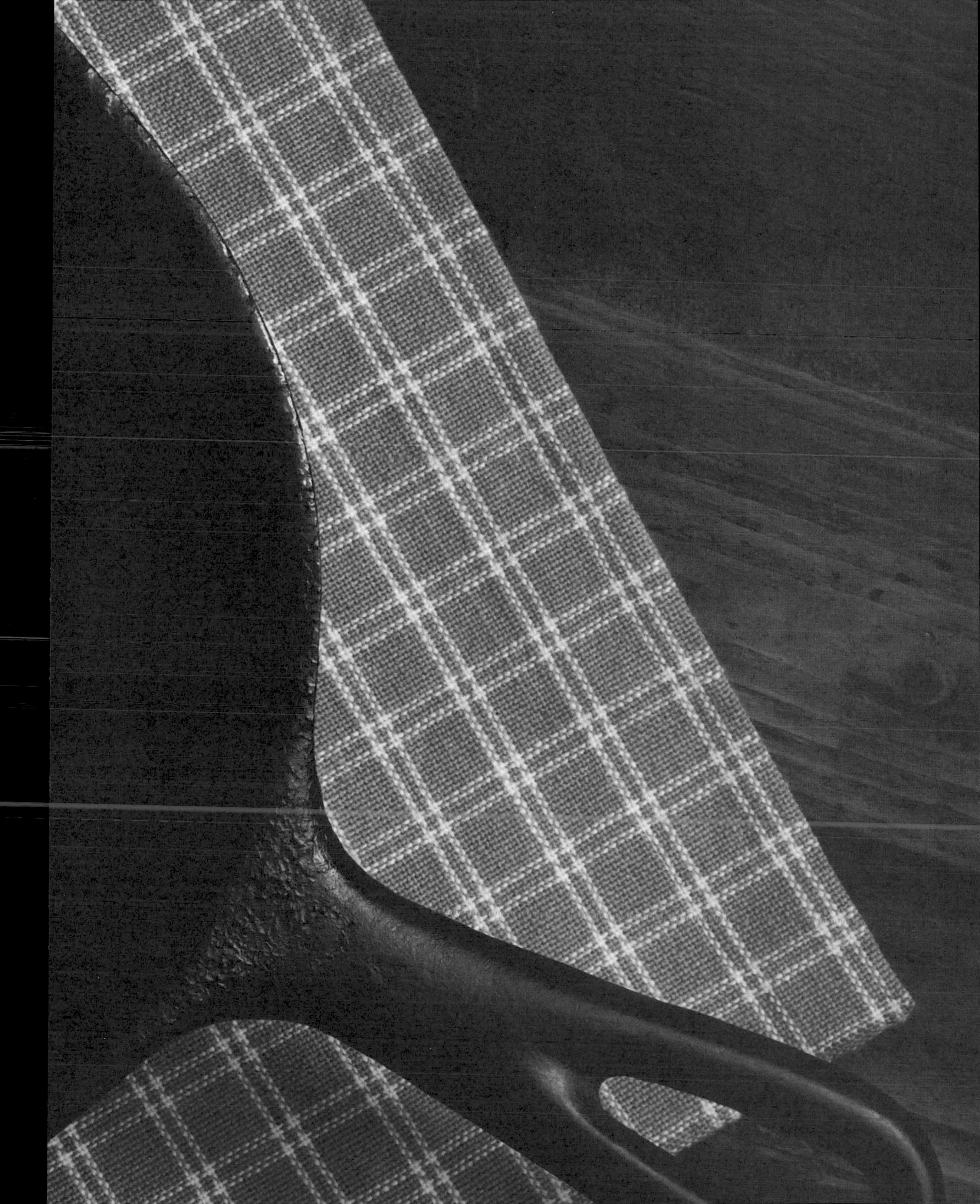

FRENCH APPLE TART

MAKES 6 TO 8 SERVINGS ✦ ACTIVE TIME: 60 MINUTES ✦ START TO FINISH: 90 MINUTES

This is the quintessential example of how the cast-iron skillet caramelizes fruits to perfection. It's what the French call "tarte tatin," and for them it's a national treasure.

1 cup flour

½ teaspoon salt

1 tablespoon sugar

6 tablespoons unsalted butter, cut into small pieces

3 tablespoons ice water

1 cup (2 sticks) unsalted butter, cut into small pieces

1½ cups sugar

8 to 10 apples, peeled, cored, and halved (see sidebar)

1. To make the pastry, whisk together the flour, salt, and sugar in a large bowl. Using your fingers, work the butter into the flour mixture until you have coarse clumps. Sprinkle the ice water over the mixture and continue to work it with your hands until it just holds together. Shape it into a ball, wrap it in plastic wrap, and refrigerate it for at least one hour but even overnight.
2. Place the pieces of butter evenly over the bottom of the skillet, then sprinkle the sugar evenly over everything. Next, start placing the apple halves in a circular pattern, starting on the outside of the pan and working in. The halves should support each other and all face the same direction. Place either one or two halves in the center when finished working around the outside. As the cake bakes, the slices will slide down a bit.
3. Place the skillet on the stove and turn the heat to medium-high. Cook the apples in the pan, uncovered, until the sugar and butter start to caramelize, about 35 minutes. While they're cooking, spoon some of the melted juices over the apples (but don't overdo it).
4. Preheat the oven to 400 degrees, and position a rack in the center.
5. Take the chilled dough out of the refrigerator and, working on a lightly floured surface, roll it out into a circle just big enough to cover the skillet (about 12 to 14 inches). Gently drape the pastry over the apples, tucking the pastry in around the sides.
6. Put the skillet in the oven and bake for about 25 minutes, until the pastry is golden brown.
7. Remove the skillet from the oven and allow to cool for about 5 minutes. Find a plate that is an inch or two larger than the top of the skillet and place it over the top. You will be inverting the tart onto the plate. Be sure to use oven mitts or secure pot holders, as the skillet will be hot.
8. Holding the plate tightly against the top of the skillet, turn the skillet over so the plate is now on the bottom. If some of the apples are stuck to the bottom, gently remove them and place them on the tart.
9. Allow to cool a few more minutes, or set aside until ready to serve (it's better if it's served warm).
10. Serve with fresh whipped cream, crème fraiche, or vanilla ice cream.

The best apples for this dessert are ones that are semi-tart and crisp. These include Mutsu, Honeycrisp, Jonagold, and Golden Delicious.

PEAR-GINGER CRUMBLE

MAKES 4 TO 6 SERVINGS ✦ ACTIVE TIME: 30 MINUTES ✦ START TO FINISH: 90 MINUTES

This is a lovely dessert to put together on a fall night, when pears are ripe and the ginger adds a deep warmth to the flavors. Serving it warm is most delicious, but if you can't, no worries—it still tastes great!

1 tablespoon butter

4 pears

1 teaspoon ginger (fresh ginger if you like the kick)

1 cup flour

½ cup dark brown sugar

1 stick chilled, unsalted butter (8 tablespoons)

½ cup rolled oats

Vanilla ice cream or whipped cream

1. Preheat oven to 350 degrees.
2. Melt 1 tablespoon butter in the skillet over medium heat.
3. Trim the tops and bottoms from the pears, cut into quarters, remove the cores, and cut each quarter in half. Lay the slices in the skillet on the melted butter. Sprinkle the pear slices with ginger. Remove from the heat.
4. In a bowl, combine the flour and brown sugar. Cut the chilled butter into slices. Using your fingers, blend the butter into the flour and sugar until coarse crumbles form. Add the rolled oats. Spread the mixture over the pears. Put the skillet in the oven and bake for 15 minutes, until the sugar is melted and bubbly. Remove from the oven and let cool for a few minutes before serving. Top with ice cream or whipped cream.

Variations

- For great gluten-free options, substitute spelt flour or almond flour for the white flour, and substitute dried, unsweetened coconut for the rolled oats.
- For a flavorful variation, add dried cherries or cranberries.
- For a lower-calorie option to the ice cream, top with Greek yogurt.

CARAMELIZED PINEAPPLE

MAKES 6 TO 8 SERVINGS ✦ ACTIVE TIME: 30 MINUTES ✦ START TO FINISH: 30 MINUTES

Experience the browned, crispy outside and the juicy inside of the pineapple. It's like a fresh fruit steak off the grill.

4 tablespoons butter

½ cup dark brown sugar

¼ cup dark rum

1 fresh pineapple, peeled, cored, and cut into ½-inch slices

1. Heat the skillet over medium-high heat. When it's hot, add the butter, sugar, and rum. Stir until the butter is melted and bubbling.
2. Add the pineapple slices to the skillet one at a time and cook until warmed through, about 2 minutes a side.
3. Keep warm in the oven on 200 degrees.

Variations

These are delicious by themselves, but there are lots of ways to dress them up and make them part of a fancier dessert.

- Put a scoop of vanilla ice cream in the hole in the center and top with a sprig of mint.
- Cut the slices into cubes and toss with chunks of mango or cantaloupe.
- Sprinkle shredded coconut over the pineapple.
- Use the pineapple as a topic for pound cake.

APPLE-PEAR CRISP

MAKES 6 TO 8 SERVINGS ✦ ACTIVE TIME: 40 MINUTES ✦ START TO FINISH: 60 MINUTES

The flavors of fall shine in this dish, which is a winner every time.

Topping

½ cup walnut pieces, preferably toasted

3 tablespoons light brown sugar

2 tablespoons butter, softened

½ teaspoon cinnamon

¼ teaspoon freshly grated nutmeg

¼ teaspoon salt

Apples & Pears

1 tablespoon butter

1 apples, peeled, cored, and sliced

1 pear, cored and sliced

1 teaspoon fresh lemon juice

1 teaspoon maple syrup

Butter pecan ice cream

1. Preheat oven to 350 degrees.
2. In a small bowl, combine the nuts, sugar, butter, cinnamon, nutmeg, and salt. Using your fingers, crumble it up until it's somewhat combined. No need to get too particular about it.
3. Heat the butter in a skillet over medium-high heat. Add the apple slices and cook, stirring gently, for a minute or so, then add the pear slices and continue to cook until the fruits soften. Sprinkle the lemon juice and maple syrup over the fruits and remove from heat.
4. Using your fingers, spread the nut/sugar mixture over the top of the fruits. Put the skillet in the oven and cook for about 10 minutes, until the fruits are bubbling and the topping is lightly toasted. Serve with butter pecan ice cream for a true taste treat.

Variations

- Instead of walnuts, use pecan pieces or crushed almonds.
- Cut the amount of nuts by half and use oatmeal for the additional amount.
- Instead of an apple-pear combo, make it with just one of these fruits, doubling up on the one you select. Add a handful of dried cranberries while the fruits are sautéeing.

BAKED APPLES

MAKES 4 SERVINGS ✦ ACTIVE TIME: 30 MINUTES ✦ START TO FINISH: 50 MINUTES

These are easy to make and are delicious served warm or at room temperature the next day. Of course, they're best with a side of vanilla ice cream or even maple Greek yogurt.

4 firm apples

2 tablespoons butter

½ cup water

Maple syrup

1. Preheat the oven to 350 degrees.
2. Peel the apples, leaving a ring of peel on the bottom where the apple will stand in the skillet. Get as much of the core out without cutting the apple in half.
3. Heat the skillet over medium-high. Add the butter and let it melt. Place the apples bottom-down in the skillet. Add the water from the center so that it distributes evenly around the apples. Drizzle the tops of the apples with maple syrup.
4. Put the skillet in the oven and cook for about 20 minutes, or until apples are soft. Drizzle with additional maple syrup if desired.

Variation

Use apple cider instead of water to make a nice apple-butter sauce, which you can simmer down after the apples are cooked to make a concentrated sauce.

BANANAS FLAMBÉ

MAKES 2 TO 4 SERVINGS ✦ ACTIVE TIME: 10 MINUTES ✦ START TO FINISH: 20 MINUTES

It's great fun to light this dessert on fire, but there's a gastronomic reason to do it, too—the intense heat caramelizes the butter and rum on the bananas. Fabulous!

2 ripe bananas (but not overly ripe, and not under-ripe)

6 tablespoons butter

¼ cup dark rum

Long matches or a lighter

1. Peel the bananas and cut them in half length-wise.
2. Heat the skillet over medium-high heat and add the butter, cooking until it melts. Lay the banana pieces on the bubbling butter and let cook about 2 minutes per side. When the bananas are softened and coated with the butter, pour the rum over them. Have someone else turn off the lights in the kitchen while you get ready to strike the match or lighter. Swirl the rum around in the pan and light it on fire. The flame will burn for just a minute or so as the alcohol burns off. When the flame dies down, the dessert is ready.
3. Put the bananas on plates with a scoop of vanilla ice cream—or put the ice cream over them in the skillet and eat out of it.

Proceed with caution on this one. The long-stemmed lighters that are made now for lighting grills and fireplaces are great for this. You want to make sure there's nothing flammable near the stove when you light the bananas. Move the bottle of rum, be sure your hair is tied back, and hold the pan with an oven mitt, not a dish towel.

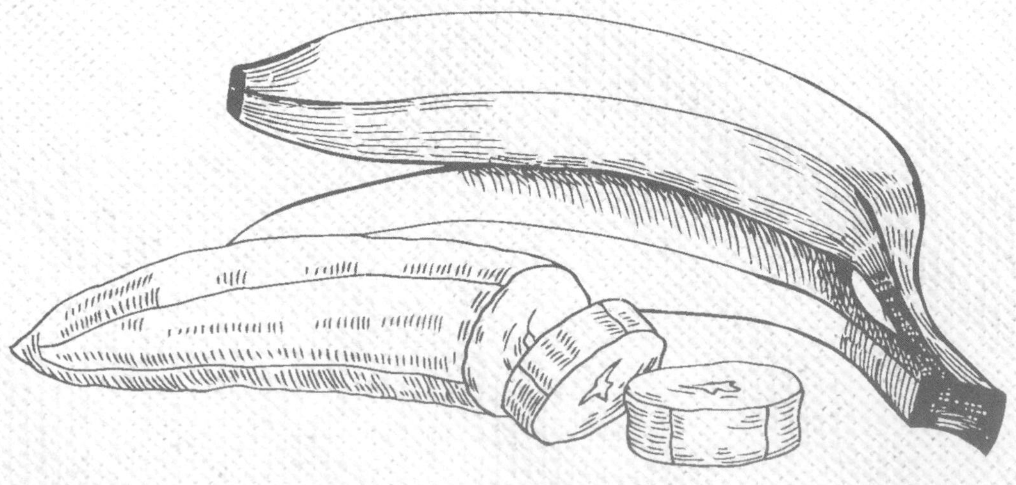

PINEAPPLE UPSIDE-DOWN CAKE

MAKES 8 TO 10 SERVINGS ✦ ACTIVE TIME: 60 MINUTES ✦ START TO FINISH: 2 HOURS

This is another recipe that is cooked to perfection in cast iron. You'll see!

Fruit

4 tablespoons butter

1 (18-oz.) can pineapple rings, plus juice

½ cup dark brown sugar

Maraschino cherries (optional)

Cake

4 tablespoons butter, chilled

1 cup light brown sugar

2 eggs

1 cup buttermilk

1 teaspoon vanilla extract

1½ cups flour

1½ teaspoons baking powder

½ teaspoon salt

1. Preheat the oven to 350 degrees.
2. Heat the skillet over medium-high heat. Add the butter, and stir in the juice from the jar of pineapples and the brown sugar. Stir continuously while the sugar melts, and continue stirring until the liquid boils and starts to thicken. Cook until the sauce turns a thick, dark, caramel consistency.
3. Remove from heat and place the pineapple rings in the liquid, working from the outside in. Place a cherry in each ring if adding cherries. Put the skillet in the oven while preparing the batter.
4. To make the cake, beat the cold butter and light brown sugar with an electric mixer until light and creamy. Beat in the eggs one at a time, making sure the first is thoroughly mixed in before adding the next.
5. In a small bowl, whisk together the flour, baking powder, and salt. Alternate adding the dry and liquid ingredients to the butter/sugar mix until all are combined but not overly smooth.
6. Remove the skillet from the oven and pour the batter over the pineapple rings. Replace in the oven and bake for 45 minutes until cake is golden and a knife inserted in the middle comes out clean.
7. Take the skillet out of the oven and let it rest for about 10 minutes.
8. Find a plate that is an inch or two larger than the top of the skillet and place it over the top. You will be inverting the cake onto the plate. Be sure to use oven mitts or secure pot holders, as the skillet will be hot. Holding the plate tightly against the top of the skillet, turn the skillet over so the plate is now on the bottom. If some of the pineapple is stuck to the bottom, gently remove it and place it on the cake.
9. Allow to cool a few more minutes, or set aside until ready to serve (it's better if it's served warm).

In 1925, Dole sponsored a pineapple recipe contest, promising to publish winning recipes in a book. It received more than 50,000 recipes, and 2,000 of them were for pineapple upside down cake. It's been a classic of American cooking ever since.

BLUEBERRY UPSIDE-DOWN CAKE

MAKES 8 TO 10 SERVINGS ✦ ACTIVE TIME: 60 MINUTES ✦ START TO FINISH: 2 HOURS

This twist on the traditional pineapple upside down cake is equally elegant and delicious.

Fruit

4 tablespoons butter

1½ cups fresh blueberries

½ cup dark brown sugar

2 tablespoons lemon juice

Cake

4 tablespoons butter, chilled

1 cup light brown sugar

2 eggs

1⅓ cups flour

1½ teaspoons baking powder

½ teaspoon salt

½ cup sour cream

¼ cup milk

1 teaspoon vanilla extract

1 teaspoon vanilla extract

1. Preheat the oven to 350 degrees.
2. Heat the skillet over medium-high heat. Add the butter. In a small bowl, gently combine the blueberries, brown sugar, and lemon juice. When the butter is melted and just bubbling, put the blueberry-sugar mix in the skillet and press the berries down into the pan. Put the skillet in the oven while preparing the batter.
3. To make the cake, beat the cold butter and light brown sugar with an electric mixer until light and creamy. Beat in the eggs one at a time, making sure the first is thoroughly mixed in before adding the next.
4. In a small bowl, whisk together the flour, baking powder, and salt. In a large measuring cup, mix the sour cream, milk, and vanilla. Alternate adding the dry and liquid ingredients to the butter/sugar mix until all are combined but not overly smooth.
5. Remove the skillet from the oven and pour the batter over the blueberries. Replace in the oven and bake for 25 minutes until cake is golden and a knife inserted in the middle comes out clean. Take the skillet out of the oven and let it rest for about 5 minutes.
6. Find a plate that is an inch or two larger than the top of the skillet and place it over the top. You will be inverting the cake onto the plate. Be sure to use oven mitts or secure pot holders, as the skillet will be hot. Holding the plate tightly against the top of the skillet, turn the skillet over so the plate is now on the bottom. If some of it is stuck to the bottom, gently remove it and place it on the cake.
7. Allow to cool a few more minutes, or set aside until ready to serve (it's better if it's served warm).

Variation

A nice sweet-tart combination is blueberries and fresh cranberries. Use 1 cup blueberries and ½ cup fresh cranberries (picked over).

RASPBERRY CORN CAKE

MAKES 4 TO 6 SERVINGS ✦ ACTIVE TIME: 40 MINUTES ✦ START TO FINISH: 60 MINUTES

The polenta in this cake gives it great texture and makes it tastier, too. It also gives the cake a lovely yellow color that highlights the raspberries.

½ cup flour

½ cup finely ground polenta

½ teaspoon baking powder

¼ teaspoon baking soda

¼ teaspoon salt

½ cup milk

¼ cup maple syrup

4 tablespoons butter, cut into pieces

½ cup fresh raspberries

1. Preheat the oven to 350 degrees. Put the skillet in the oven to get it hot.
2. In a bowl, mix the flour, polenta, baking powder, baking soda, and salt. In another bowl, whisk together the milk and syrup. Stir the wet ingredients into the dry ingredients and combine thoroughly but not overly.
3. Using oven mitts or potholders, remove the hot skillet from the oven and add the pieces of butter. Pour the batter over the butter, and sprinkle the raspberries on top.
4. Put the skillet back in the oven and bake for about 20 minutes, until just set and golden, and a toothpick inserted in the middle comes out clean. Serve with vanilla ice cream and additional berries.

Variations

- Substitute fresh blueberries, black berries, or even strawberries for the raspberries.
- For added texture and crunch, sprinkle some polenta over the top of the cake before putting it back in the oven.
- Add ¼ cup dried organic coconut and an additional ¼ cup of milk.
- Substitute unsweetened almond milk for the regular milk.
- Substitute vanilla almond milk for the milk, adding ¼ cup more and omitting the maple syrup (vanilla almond milk is sweet).

NEW ENGLAND SPIDER CAKE

MAKES 4 TO 6 SERVINGS ✦ ACTIVE TIME: 30 MINUTES ✦ START TO FINISH: 40 MINUTES

Early settlers in New England used a version of today's cast-iron skillet that had legs on it so it could sit in the fire. While this is essentially a recipe for corn bread, made and cooked this way the outside becomes crisp and the inside forms a custardy layer.

1¼ cups yellow corn meal

½ cup sugar

1 teaspoon baking soda

1 teaspoon salt

2 cups buttermilk

2 large eggs

2 tablespoons unsalted butter

1. Preheat oven to 400 degrees and position a rack in the middle.
2. In a large bowl, combine the corn meal, sugar, baking soda, and salt. In a separate bowl, beat the eggs with the buttermilk until thoroughly combined. Gradually add it to the cornmeal mixture.
3. Heat the skillet over high heat and add the butter. When melted and swirled around to cover the whole bottom, pour in the batter.
4. Transfer the skillet to the oven and bake about 20 minutes, until the cake is golden brown and springy to the touch. Melt some additional butter on the surface when you take it out of the oven, and serve with jam, fresh berries, or maple syrup.

GIANT CHOCOLATE CHIP COOKIE

MAKES 1 LARGE COOKIE ✦ ACTIVE TIME: 20 MINUTES ✦ START TO FINISH: 45 MINUTES

Yes, your cast iron skillet is also a great baking sheet—just smaller, and with sides. So why not cook a giant cookie in it? Here's how.

1 cup butter, softened

½ cup white sugar

1 cup brown sugar

2 eggs

2 teaspoons vanilla extract

1 teaspoon baking soda

2 teaspoons hot water

½ teaspoon salt

2½ cups flour

2 cups semisweet chocolate chips

1. Preheat oven to 375 degrees. Heat the skillet in the oven while making the batter.
2. In a large bowl, cream together the butter and sugars. Add the eggs one at a time, being sure to combine thoroughly before proceeding. Stir in the vanilla.
3. Dissolve the baking soda in the hot water and add to the batter along with the salt. Stir in the flour and chocolate chips.
4. Remove the skillet from the oven and put the batter in it, smoothing the top with a spatula.
5. Put the skillet in the oven and cook until golden, about 15 minutes. Serve with ice cream.

Variation

If you like nuts in your chocolate chip cookies, you can add them here. Mix in ½ cup walnut or almond pieces when adding the flour and chocolate chips.

APPLE PIE

MAKES 6 TO 8 SERVINGS ✦ ACTIVE TIME: 1 HOUR ✦ START TO FINISH: 2 HOURS

Impress your friends! Impress your family! Impress yourself—you won't believe how easy this is and how delicious the result!

4 pounds Granny Smith apples

1 teaspoon ground cinnamon

¾ cup sugar

1 teaspoon lemon juice

½ cup butter

1 cup light brown sugar

1 (14.1-oz.) package refrigerated piecrusts

1 egg white

2 tablespoons sugar

1. Preheat the oven to 350 degrees.
2. Peel and core the apples, and cut into ½-inch-thick wedges. Toss apples with cinnamon, sugar, and lemon juice.
3. Put the skillet over medium heat and melt the butter in it. Add the brown sugar and cook, stirring constantly, until sugar is dissolved, one or two minutes. Remove pan from heat.
4. Place 1 of the piecrusts over the sugar mixture. Fill with the apple/spice mix, and place the other crust over the apples, crimping the edges together.
5. Brush the top crust with the egg white, and sprinkle the sugar over it. Cut 4 or 5 slits in the middle.
6. Put the skillet in the oven and bake for 60 to 70 minutes until golden brown and bubbly. Cover the outermost edge with aluminum foil in the last 10 minutes of baking to prevent it from burning.
7. Allow to cool before serving. Serve with whipped cream or ice cream.

You can flavor whipped cream with liqueur for an especially yummy topping. Beat heavy or whipping cream until soft peaks form. Add about 1/4 cup sugar and continue beating until stiff peaks form. Gently beat in 1/4 cup liqueur, such as apple brandy or Cointreau.

STRAWBERRY RHUBARB CRISP

MAKES 4 SERVINGS ✦ ACTIVE TIME: 30 MINUTES ✦ START TO FINISH: 60 MINUTES

Nothing says early summer like fresh, juicy strawberries. Rhubarb contributes texture and tartness to cooked strawberries. Together, they're magic.

1½ cups rhubarb, cut into ½-inch pieces

1½ cups strawberries, sliced

2 tablespoons sugar

2 teaspoons flour

4 tablespoons butter, chilled, cut into pieces

¼ cup dark brown sugar

¾ cup oats (quick cooking but not instant)

⅓ cup flour

1. Preheat oven to 450 degrees.
2. In a bowl, combine the rhubarb pieces, strawberry slices, sugar, and flour, and toss to coat the fruit. Transfer to the skillet.
3. In another bowl, work the butter in with the sugar using a fork. Add the oats and flour and continue to work with the fork to create a crumbly mix. Sprinkle it over the fruit in the skillet.
4. Put the skillet in the oven and bake for about 30 minutes until the topping is golden and the fruit is bubbly. Serve warm with whipped cream or ice cream.

In the early 1900s, American rhubarb farmers successfully lobbied for their vegetable to be officially designated as a fruit so that they could get lower tax rates and less stringent interstate shipping laws.

Cast-iron skillets are the perfect tools for making breads and other sweet treats. They heat evenly, which allows them to brown crusts consistently and produce fluffy pastries.

PEACH CRISP

MAKES 4 TO 6 SERVINGS ✦ ACTIVE TIME: 30 MINUTES ✦ START TO FINISH: 60 MINUTES

Just like a strawberry-rhubarb crisp says early summer, so a fresh peach crisp says late summer. Use ripe fruit and plenty of it and you may want to make this every night while peaches are in season.

5 or 6 peaches, pitted and sliced (skin on or off)

¼ cup sugar to mix with peaches

1 to 2 tablespoons flour

¾ cup flour

¼ teaspoon salt

½ cup sugar for the topping

¼ cup dark brown sugar

8 tablespoons chilled butter, cut into pieces

½ cup oats (quick-cooking but not instant)

1. Preheat oven to 350 degrees.
2. In a bowl, combine peach slices with sugar and flour. The amount of flour you use will depend on how juicy the peaches are; more juice means more flour. Let the peaches sit in the bowl while you make the topping. If there's juice in the bowl after sitting, add another tablespoon of flour.
3. In another bowl, make the topping. Blend the flour, salt, and both sugars together, and add the butter, using a fork to combine them. When somewhat mixed and crumbly, add the oats and stir. The topping should be crumbly.
4. Put the peaches in the skillet and top with the crumbly dough.
5. Put in the oven and bake for about 1 hour until the topping is golden and the peaches are bubbling. If it doesn't look crispy enough, turn the oven up to 375 degrees and continue to bake, checking every 5 minutes until it looks just right. Be careful not to burn the topping.
6. Serve warm with fresh whipped cream and a sprinkling of toasted nuts.

Variation

Many fruit crisp recipes feature nuts in the topping. These can be whatever you like: walnuts, pecans, or almonds. Break the raw nuts into pieces and use about ½ cup in the topping.

LEMON CAKE

MAKES 6 TO 8 SERVINGS ✦ ACTIVE TIME: 40 MINUTES ✦ START TO FINISH: 90 MINUTES

Fragrant, moist, and bursting with the flavor of fresh lemons, this is a delightful dessert or snack.

¾ cup sugar

Zest of two lemons (about 1 tablespoon)

6 tablespoons butter, cut in pieces

2 eggs

1 cup flour

1 teaspoon baking powder

½ cup milk

1. Preheat oven to 350 degrees.
2. In a large bowl, combine the sugar and lemon zest, working them together so the zest penetrates the sugar. Add the butter, and cream the butter and lemon-sugar together until light. Add the eggs one at a time, combining thoroughly after each addition.
3. In the measuring cup you use for the flour, add the baking powder and mix the dry ingredients together. Alternately add the flour mix and the milk to the butter-sugar mix until thoroughly combined.
4. Grease the skillet with some butter and add the cake batter.
5. Put in the oven and bake for about 30 to 35 minutes, until the top is golden and the cake springs to the touch and a toothpick inserted in the middle comes out clean. Cool and cut into wedges.

Variations

This cake is delicious on its own, but it can be topped with all kinds of treats. Consider these:

- Fresh-squeezed lemon juice and granulated sugar
- Whipped cream
- Fresh fruit like raspberries, strawberries, blueberries, blackberries, or a combination of berries
- Ice cream (almost any flavor)
- Pecans sautéed in butter and brown sugar

DUTCH APPLE BABY

SERVES 4 ✦ ACTIVE TIME: 45 MINUTES ✦ START TO FINISH: 75 MINUTES

This is a classic cast-iron skillet recipe for a pastry that puffs in the oven is reminiscent of the recipe for Eyre's pancakes in the Breakfast chapter.

2 firm, semi-tart apples, like Mutsu or Golden Delicious

4 tablespoons butter

¼ cup sugar

1 tablespoon cinnamon

3 tablespoons sugar

¾ cup flour

¼ teaspoon salt

¾ cup milk

4 eggs

1 teaspoon vanilla or almond extract

Confectioner's sugar for dusting

1. Preheat the oven to 425 degrees and position a rack in the middle.
2. Peel and core the apples, and cut into slices. Heat a skillet over medium-high heat. Add the butter and apples and cook, stirring, for 3 to 4 minutes until the apples soften. Add the sugar and cinnamon and continue cooking for another 3 or 4 minutes. Distribute the apples evenly over the bottom of the skillet and remove from heat.
3. In a large bowl, mix the flour and salt. In a smaller bowl, whisk together the milk, eggs, and vanilla or almond extract. Add the wet ingredients to the dry ingredients and stir to combine. Pour the batter over the apples.
4. Put the skillet in the oven and bake for 15 to 20 minutes until the "baby" is puffed and browned on the top.
5. Remove from the oven and allow to cool for a few minutes. Run a knife along the edge of the skillet to loosen the dessert. Put a plate over the skillet and, using oven mitts or pot holders, flip the skillet over so the dessert is transferred to the plate. Serve warm with a dusting of confectioner's sugar.

The Dutch Apple Baby is attributed to early Pennsylvania Dutch settlers.

CHOCOLATE CAKE

SERVES 4 ✦ ACTIVE TIME: 20 MINUTES ✦ START TO FINISH: 60 MINUTES

This is another winner that you'll want to serve again and again either plain or with a topping of your choice. Who doesn't appreciate chocolate cake?

6 tablespoons butter, cut in pieces

1 cup sugar

2 eggs

½ teaspoon vanilla extract

1 cup flour

1 teaspoon baking powder

2 tablespoons unsweetened cocoa powder

½ cup milk

1. Preheat oven to 350 degrees.
2. In a large bowl, cream the butter and sugar together until light. Add the eggs one at a time, combining thoroughly after each addition. Stir in the vanilla extract.
3. In a small bowl, combine the flour, baking powder, and cocoa powder, and mix the dry ingredients together. Alternately add the flour mix and the milk to the butter-sugar mix until thoroughly combined.
4. Grease the skillet with some butter and add the cake batter.
5. Put in the oven and bake for about 30 to 35 minutes, until the top is golden and the cake springs to the touch and a toothpick inserted in the middle comes out clean. Cool and cut into wedges.

Variations

There are so many ways to top this simple chocolate cake, including whipped cream, frosting, fresh berries, berries and cream, chocolate syrup, ice cream (almost any flavor), or marshmallow fluff.

CHERRY CLAFOUTI

MAKES 4 TO 6 SERVINGS **ACTIVE TIME: 20 MINUTES** **START TO FINISH: 45 MINUTES**

Another French specialty that originated in the Limousin region and used the sour cherries that grew there, this dessert is so delicious that it is now known around the world. It's essentially full-flavored cherries baked in a custard. How can you go wrong?

8 tablespoons butter, melted

½ cup sugar

⅔ cup flour

½ teaspoon salt

1 teaspoon vanilla extract

3 eggs, beaten

1 cup milk

2 tablespoons unsalted butter

3 cups ripe cherries (pits in)

½ cup + 2 teaspoons sugar

Preheat oven to 400 degrees.

In a large bowl, mix together 6 tablespoons of the butter, sugar, flour, salt, vanilla, eggs, and milk until all ingredients are blended and smooth. Set aside.

Put 2 tablespoons of butter in the skillet and put it in the oven to heat up.

Transfer the skillet to the stovetop and add the additional butter. When it is melted, put the sugar in the skillet and shake it so it distributes evenly. Add the cherries. Pour the batter over the cherries, sprinkle with the last teaspoons of sugar, and put the skillet back in the oven. Bake for about 30 minutes, or until the topping is golden brown and set in the center.

Serve warm—and be sure to let diners know that the cherries contain their pits

The Limousin region of France is located in the center of the country, with Bordeaux to the west and Lyon to the east. Limoges is the largest city in the region. It is known for its agricultural heritage, including the griottes (sour morello cherries) grown there. There is some debate about whether the pits should be removed from the cherries before baking, but even Julia Child left them in, going with the belief that the pits add flavor.

PEAR CLAFOUTI

MAKES 4 TO 6 SERVINGS ✦ ACTIVE TIME: 20 MINUTES ✦ START TO FINISH: 45 MINUTES

When you get the hang of making clafouti, you'll want to experiment making it with different fruits. This one is made with pears and instead of vanilla extract has almond extract to accentuate their mild nuttiness.

8 tablespoons melted butter

½ cup sugar

⅔ cup flour

½ teaspoon salt

1 teaspoon almond extract

3 eggs

1 cup milk

4 tablespoons unsalted butter

4 pears

½ cup + 2 teaspoons sugar

1. Preheat oven to 400 degrees.
2. In a large bowl, mix together 6 tablespoons of the butter, sugar, flour, salt, almond extract, eggs, and milk until all ingredients are blended and smooth. Set aside.
3. Put 2 tablespoons of butter in the cast-iron skillet and put it in the oven to heat up.
4. In another skillet on the stove, working over medium-high heat, add the additional butter until melted. Add the fruit and sugar to the butter and cook, stirring, until the pears are just soft and glazed, about 3 minutes.
5. Remove the skillet from the oven and pour in half the batter. Spoon the cooked pears over the batter, and then add the remaining batter. Sprinkle with the sugar.
6. Bake in the oven for 25 to 30 minutes until the clafouti is golden brown and set in the center. Serve warm with whipped cream or confectioner's sugar if desired, or just by itself.

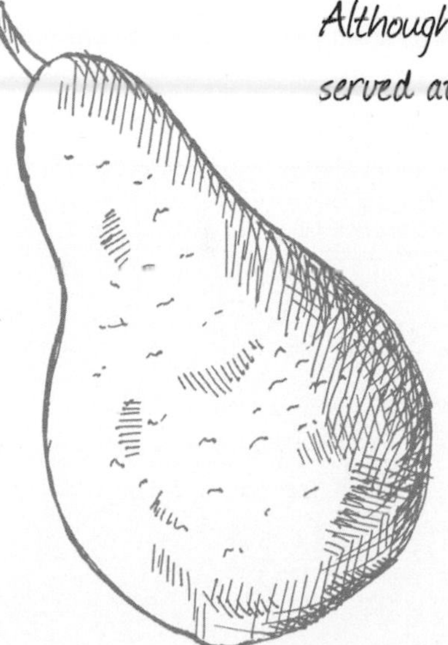

Although clafouti is most delicious served warm, it is plenty tasty served at room temperature or even chilled.

BREAD PUDDING

MAKES 8 TO 10 SERVINGS ✦ ACTIVE TIME: 1 HOUR ✦ START TO FINISH: 2 HOURS

Whoever invented bread pudding was on to something—use up some slightly stale bread, drench it in butter, sugar, and eggs, and bake. It's a bit trickier than that, but not much. Enjoy!

6 tablespoons butter

1 large baguette, cubed preferably a day old

¼ cup raisins (optional)

⅔ cup toasted almonds or walnuts (optional)

1 cup apples or pears, cored and diced

3 eggs

1½ cups milk

1½ cups heavy cream

1 cup sugar

1 tablespoon vanilla extract

¼ teaspoon cinnamon

⅛ teaspoon nutmeg

⅛ teaspoon ginger

1. Prepare the skillet by coating it with 2 tablespoons of the butter. Make a layer of bread cubes using half the baguette. Sprinkle half of the raisins, nuts, and fruit over the cubes, and make another layer, starting with the bread cubes and topping with the raisins, nuts, and fruit.
2. In a large bowl, whisk the eggs until frothy and add the milk, cream, sugar, vanilla, and spices. Whisk briskly to blend thoroughly. Pour the mixture over the bread layers, shaking the pan slightly to be sure to distribute throughout and so that the top cubes are just moistened while the bottom layer gets most of the liquid.
3. Refrigerate for about an hour, pressing down on the bread occasionally.
4. Preheat the oven to 325 degrees and position a rack in the center. Before putting the skillet in the oven, cut up the remaining 4 tablespoons of butter into little pieces and place them over the top of the pudding. Bake in the oven for 1 hour.
5. Remove and allow to cool for about a half hour. Serve with fresh whipped cream, ice cream, or a Grand Marnier sauce (see below).

GRAND MARNIER SAUCE

6 tablespoons butter

½ cup sugar

½ cup Grand Marnier

1 egg

1. Melt the butter in a heavy-bottomed saucepan over medium heat. Add the sugar and stir constantly with a wooden spoon while it dissolves and begins to cook. Stir until dissolved, about 2 minutes, then stir in the Grand Marnier, continue to cook for a minute or two, and remove from the heat.
2. In a bowl, whisk the egg until frothy. Add a large spoonful of the warm Grand Marnier/sugar sauce to the egg and continue to whisk so that it combines. Transfer this to the saucepan and whisk it in with the rest of the sauce.
3. On low heat, cook the sauce, whisking constantly, until it starts to thicken (about 3 minutes). Remove from the heat and continue to whisk as it thickens. Drizzle it over bread pudding, or serve on the side.

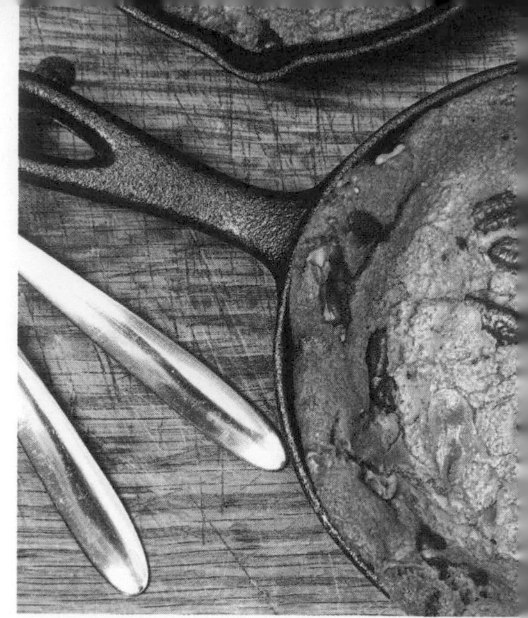

METRIC CONVERSION CHART

US measurement	Approximate metric liquid measurement	Approximate metric dry measurement
1 teaspoon	5 mL	
1 tablespoon or ½ ounce	15 mL	14 g
1 ounce or ⅛ cup	30 mL	29 g
¼ cup or 2 ounces	60 mL	57 g
⅓ cup	80 mL	
½ cup or 4 ounces	120 mL	¼ pound/ 113 g
⅔ cup	160 mL	
¾ cup or 6 ounces	180 mL	
1 cup or 8 ounces or ½ pint	240 mL	½ pound/ 227 g
1 ½ cups or 12 ounces	350 mL	
2 cups or 1 pint or 16 ounces	475 mL	1 pound/ 454 g
3 cups or 1 ½ pints	700 mL	
4 cups or 2 pints or 1 quart	950 mL	

INDEX

A

B

C

D

E

F

G

H

I

J

L

ABOUT APPLESEED PRESS BOOK PUBLISHERS

Great ideas grow over time. From seed to harvest, Appleseed Press brings fine reading and entertainment together between the covers of its creatively crafted books. Our grove bears fruit twice a year, publishing a new crop of titles each spring and fall.

Visit us online at
appleseedpressbooks.com
or write to us at
68 North Street
Kennebunkport, Maine 04046